T0312319

Cambridge Elements ≡

Elements in Ancient Philosophy
edited by
James Warren
University of Cambridge

CONTEMPLATION AND CIVIC HAPPINESS IN PLATO AND ARISTOTLE

Dominic Scott
University of Oxford

CAMBRIDGE
UNIVERSITY PRESS

CAMBRIDGE
UNIVERSITY PRESS

Shaftesbury Road, Cambridge CB2 8EA, United Kingdom

One Liberty Plaza, 20th Floor, New York, NY 10006, USA

477 Williamstown Road, Port Melbourne, VIC 3207, Australia

314–321, 3rd Floor, Plot 3, Splendor Forum, Jasola District Centre,
New Delhi – 110025, India

103 Penang Road, #05–06/07, Visioncrest Commercial, Singapore 238467

Cambridge University Press is part of Cambridge University Press & Assessment,
a department of the University of Cambridge.

We share the University's mission to contribute to society through the pursuit of
education, learning and research at the highest international levels of excellence.

www.cambridge.org
Information on this title: www.cambridge.org/9781009539326

DOI: 10.1017/9781009372602

First published 2024

A catalogue record for this publication is available from the British Library

ISBN 978-1-009-53932-6 Hardback
ISBN 978-1-009-37259-6 Paperback
ISSN 2631-4118 (online)
ISSN 2631-410X (print)

Contemplation and Civic Happiness in Plato and Aristotle

Elements in Ancient Philosophy

DOI: 10.1017/9781009372602
First published online: December 2024

Dominic Scott
University of Oxford
Author for correspondence: Dominic Scott, dominic.scott@philosophy.ox.ac.uk

Abstract: This study concerns the civic value of contemplation in Plato and Aristotle: how does intellectual contemplation contribute to the happiness of the ideal state? The texts discussed include the *Republic, the Nicomachean Ethics* and the *Politics,* works in which contemplation is viewed from a political angle. The Element concludes that in the *Republic* contemplation has purely instrumental value, whereas in the *Politics* and *Nicomachean Ethics* it has purely intrinsic value. To do justice to the complexity of the issues involved, the author addresses a broader question about the nature of civic happiness: whether it is merely the aggregate of individual happiness or an organic quality that arises from the structure of the state. Answering this question has implications for how contemplation contributes to civic happiness. The study also discusses how many citizens Plato and Aristotle expected to be engaged in contemplation in the ideal state.

Keywords: Plato, Aristotle, Contemplation, Happiness, Politics

Isbns: 9781009539326 (HB), 9781009372596 (PB), 9781009372602 (OC)
Issns: 2631-4118 (online), 2631-410X (print)

Contents

1 Introduction

Plato and Aristotle both treat intellectual contemplation (*theōria*) as the highest form of happiness (*eudaimonia*) possible for a human being. Plato does so in a number of dialogues (e.g. the *Phaedo, Symposium, Republic* and *Phaedrus*), Aristotle in the last book of the *Nicomachean Ethics*. This means that studying their approaches to contemplation typically involves an ethical focus. For instance, given the enormous value that contemplation has for the individual, what place is left in their life for the moral virtues of justice, courage and temperance? In this study, however, I shall examine contemplation from a political perspective, in the sense of looking at its civic value: even if it counts as a good for the individual, how does the state benefit from having a number of citizens contemplating? The texts on which I shall focus are the *Republic*, the *Nicomachean Ethics* and the *Politics*, works in which contemplation is viewed from a political angle as well as an individual one.

Initially, I shall tackle this question through the distinction between intrinsic and instrumental value: when looking at the issue from the perspective of social benefit, did Plato and Aristotle attribute both kinds of value to contemplation or only one of them? But to do justice to the complexity of the issue, we also need to address a broader question about the nature of civic *eudaimonia*: whether it is merely the aggregate of individual happiness or an organic quality that arises from the structure of the state. On the aggregative view, it is easy to see how individual contemplation contributes to civic *eudaimonia*: simply by having a number of citizens engaged in contemplation, one can in principle increase the overall happiness of the state (and the more people who contemplate, the happier the city). Seen in this way, contemplation is a component of civic happiness, something intrinsically good for the state, whether or not it has instrumental value as well.

In Section 2, however, I argue that Plato espoused an organic account of civic happiness and analysed it in terms of unity, harmony and proportion. This affects his stance on whether contemplation has intrinsic value for the state. He clearly believes that it is both instrumentally and intrinsically good for the individual; also, that it is instrumentally good for the state, as his defence of philosopher-rulers shows. But, because he associates civic happiness with structural properties like unity, contemplation is not a component of that happiness, but a means towards achieving it (through the activity of the philosopher-rulers). So, from the point of view of the state, it has only instrumental value.

In Section 3, I turn to Aristotle, who is quite clear that, for the individual, contemplation has only intrinsic value. If it also has value for the state – which it must, given that it is the task of the statesman to promote it – such value must also be intrinsic. But how exactly does it contribute intrinsic value to the state? To answer this question, I turn again to the distinction between organic and aggregative accounts of civic happiness. Aristotle explicitly rejects Plato's account of civic happiness as unity in *Pol.* II 5. But it does not follow from this that he rejected any form of the organic conception. The starting point for understanding his position on this issue is his claim that civic happiness is the same for the state as for the individual. This means that we can turn to his definition of individual happiness to throw light on its civic form. We know that he defines *eudaimonia* as activity in accordance with virtue. But at the end of the *NE*, he distinguishes two forms, the activity of theoretical reason (perfect *eudaimonia*) and the activity of practical reason and the moral virtues (secondary *eudaimonia*). So civic happiness will follow suit: one form will involve the activity of contemplation within the state, the other requires activity in accordance with practical reason and the moral virtue. Whether he treats *eudaimonia* as organic or aggregative depends on the nature of the virtuous activities involved. Secondary *eudaimonia* involves structured relations between different groups in the state, primarily the rulers and the subjects, just as secondary *eudaimonia* in the individual involves the correct interactions between the relevant parts of the soul. (Aristotle, I shall argue, exploits his own version of Plato's state-soul parallel in developing this idea.) So civic *eudaimonia* of the secondary form is organic. But contemplation, the activity of theoretical reason, is a simpler affair: it is more solitary than collaborative. A 'contemplative' state is simply one in which a number of individual citizens are encouraged and enabled to practise contemplation. For this kind of *eudaimonia*, the aggregative account is more appropriate. There is no contradiction here, because Aristotle has two very different forms of *eudaimonia*, one involving a high degree of structure, the other not. Once we are clear on this, we can conclude that contemplation is intrinsically good for the state in the manner described earlier: the contemplative activities of individual citizens are components of the aggregate *eudaimonia*.

In Section 4, I turn to a related question. For a state to derive value from contemplation, how many citizens need to be contemplating – just a select few, or a much broader swathe of society? In Plato's case, the answer is clear enough: only a very few citizens, the philosopher-rulers, will engage in contemplation. But the issue is much more difficult where Aristotle is concerned. There are signs from his discussion of contemplation in *Politics* VII that he thought it should be widely practised in the state. And yet, to judge from remarks in the *NE*, it is a highly recherché activity involving the study of metaphysical theology, which is surely only possible for a few. The purpose of Section 4 is to show how Aristotle resolved this tension.

2 Plato on the Social Value of Contemplation

2.1 Preliminaries

In the context of the *Republic*, I shall take contemplation to involve knowledge of forms – knowledge that Socrates terms *noēsis* in his image of the divided line (VI 511d8).[1] The objects of contemplation therefore include all the examples of forms that we are given in the central books of the *Republic*: goodness (506b2–509b9), beauty (476b9–480a13 and 501b2), justice and temperance (501b2), as well as largeness and smallness (523e1–524c11). The form of the good plays a pivotal role, providing the first principle in terms of which the other forms are understood.

There are two distinctions to bear in mind here. First, although contemplation and *noēsis* are intimately connected, they are not identical: contemplation requires the act of focusing upon knowledge (whether it is being used it for practical ends or not). Put in these terms, my main interest will be in the value of actualising *noēsis*, not merely in its possession.[2] Second, while perfect contemplation involves *noēsis*, there might be imperfect types that involve lesser cognitive states. At one point, for instance, Plato uses the language of contemplation in connection with mathematical understanding (*dianoia*), the state that stands immediately below *noēsis* on the divided line.[3] Another example of imperfect contemplation would be thinking about forms without yet having apprehended the nature of the good. This level of attainment is reached when the trainee guardians study dialectic between the ages of thirty and thirty-five. They only acquire knowledge of the good at fifty, which is when perfect contemplation becomes possible for them. In what follows, my main interest will be in the activity of perfect contemplation and its value for the state, but at certain points I shall discuss the value of forms of contemplation that fall short of the ideal.

Of course, the *Republic* is not the only dialogue in which Plato discusses contemplation. There is a particularly lyrical description in the *Phaedrus*, in which the souls of the gods, and even of some humans, journey to a place beyond the heavens. Here they are moved in a circle and watch the spectacle of the forms (247c3–248a5). In our earthly life, we can but glimpse flashes of beauty to aid our recollection of that discarnate vision. The *Phaedo* also talks of

---

[1] Plato uses the term *theōria* to refer to contemplation of forms at *Rep.* VII 517d5. He also uses the verb 'contemplate' (*theōrein*) in relation to the forms at *Phaedrus* 247c1 and d4.

[2] This distinction is made explicitly in *Theaet.* 197b9–198b7. It is, of course, well-known in Aristotle. See *NE* VII 3, 1146b31–4, *An.* II 1, 412a22–7, *Met.* IX 6, 1048a32–5, and *Phys.* VIII 4, 255a33–4.

[3] *Rep.* VI 511c4–8; cf. also 486a8. For another example of contemplation being used of a cognitive state that falls short of knowledge of forms, see *Symp.* 210d4.

contemplation in relation to the afterlife and sounds sceptical as to whether we can attain knowledge of forms in our earthly existence. Finally, the *Symposium*, like the *Phaedrus*, focuses on contemplation of the form of beauty, but talks as if we can attain knowledge of it even in this life (212a2–7).

The *Republic* also seems optimistic about the chances of at least some humans acquiring knowledge of forms in this life. But what distinguishes its treatment of contemplation from these other dialogues is the political context: contemplation is something promoted by and for the ideal state. Hence our main question: what kind of value does contemplation bring to the city that sponsors it?

To answer this question, I shall start with the well-known distinction between instrumental and intrinsic value. This distinction appears early in *Republic* II, where Glaucon challenges Socrates to show that justice is not merely good for its consequences, but also in itself (357b4–358a3). Assuming this distinction, he marks out three types of good: things that have only intrinsic value, things that have only instrumental value, and things that have both. As we attempt to pin down the kind of value that contemplation has for the state, it will be relatively easy to show that it has instrumental value. The challenge will be to show whether it also has intrinsic value. Ultimately, I shall argue that it does not. Such value applies only at the level of the individual.

Before we discuss the civic value of contemplation, it will help to ask about its value for the individual. As we shall see, answering this question involves less controversy than the political case, and some of what can be said of the individual can easily be applied to the state.

2.2 The Individual: Intrinsic and Instrumental Value

It is uncontroversial to say that the contemplation of forms is intrinsically good for the individual. In the *Republic*, this is clear from the famous passage about the return to the cave (VII 519d4–521b11): the philosophers appear reluctant to return and rule the city because they would much rather stay in 'the isles of the blest' (519c5; cf. 540b6). The assumption underlying this whole passage is, of course, that contemplation is the activity of supreme happiness. This also coheres with passages in other dialogues, such as the *Phaedo, Symposium* and *Phaedrus*, which place philosophical contemplation at the apex of human life, even as something divine, or at least akin to the divine.[4]

What about instrumental value? There is no doubt that using one's knowledge of forms is essential for leading the truly good and just life. Plato's view is that

---

[4] *Phaedo* 81a4–10, *Symposium* 212a5–7 and *Phaedrus* 248a2. The *Republic* makes the connection with divinity at VI 500c3–d3.

such knowledge can be applied in practical decision-making. Whether the outcome of this application involves a *bona fide* case of knowledge is a famously disputed question.[5] Perhaps true knowledge can only be of forms. Even so, philosophers who apply their knowledge of forms to particulars will still be far better at practical decision-making than those ignorant of the forms.

However, this establishes only the instrumental value of contemplative knowledge, not of contemplative activity. Imagine a philosopher who attains knowledge of the good and, with it, full knowledge of the other forms. They are now able to engage in perfect contemplation. But when they do so, will they accrue instrumental benefit, or does such benefit only arise when they abstain from pure contemplation and apply their knowledge to practical decision making?

One way to show that contemplation has instrumental value is to focus on its relation to pleasure. Actively contemplating the forms, even without any thought for practical decision-making, produces pleasures of the greatest and purest kind, as Socrates attempts to establish towards the end of book IX (583b2–588a10).

There is another way in which contemplation could have instrumental value for the individual. At the beginning of book VI, Socrates argues that, in addition to having the capacity for true knowledge, philosophers naturally possess a range of moral qualities that sound very much like virtues (484a1–487a5). The philosophical mindset is relatively disinterested in material pleasures, which leads it to become temperate; it is also just, because such a person will lack incentives to renege on their agreements. Since philosophers contemplate 'all time and all being',[6] they acquire grandness of perspective or vision; from such a perspective, even death seems a small matter, so they are also rendered courageous. On this argument, therefore, sustained contemplation is useful by generating a whole string of moral virtues.

This sounds like clear evidence for the instrumental value of contemplation. But there is a complication. When Socrates talks of the philosopher here, he is probably not thinking, first and foremost, of someone who has acquired full philosophical knowledge, but of someone in the process of acquiring it. The character whom Socrates is discussing, someone who has a philosophical nature, possesses that nature 'from youth onwards' (εὐθὺς νέου ὄντος, 486b10–11). This nature reveals gradually itself through the love of learning, not about the world of

---

[5] Much of the debate centres on the interpretation of *Rep*. V 476a1–480a13, where Socrates seems to argue that knowledge is only of forms, belief only of particulars. This reading has been disputed by Fine (1990) esp. 87–95. Also relevant is VII 520c4, which seems to suggest that the philosopher who returns to the cave will have knowledge of particulars, not just forms. Fine leans heavily on this passage, though Sedley (2007) 260–61 disputes her reading.

[6] 486a8–9: μεγαλοπρέπεια καὶ θεωρία παντὸς μὲν χρόνου.

becoming but of being. As this desire starts to become satisfied, the qualities just mentioned, such as temperance and courage, emerge – and they do so while the person is young (485d3–4). Socrates must be thinking of someone intellectually precocious, who shows an intense curiosity quite early in life about being rather than becoming. The qualities termed temperance, justice, magnanimity and courage start to arise the more they satisfy this curiosity, because their desires for physical pleasures diminish and their vision becomes increasingly broad. However, not yet being backed by fully fledged knowledge, these are not full-blown virtues, but qualities that will eventually grow into the virtues.[7] Strictly speaking, therefore, this passage tells us that 'imperfect' contemplation or, perhaps, inquiry into forms, will be useful in generating certain qualities of character;[8] it is not primarily talking about perfect contemplation, that is, the actualisation of full knowledge. Such contemplation does not actually *produce* such qualities. What we can say, however, is that continued contemplation in the full sense helps to maintain the qualities (which are by now *bona fide* virtues) and keep them locked in place. This would constitute a further instrumental value, still from the point of view of the individual.

One might think that, once a philosopher has acquired the virtues, they can never be erased. In the passage we have just discussed from book VI, Socrates talks of the philosopher who achieves 'perfection'.[9] In terms of the curriculum that he will go on to unveil in book VII, this is someone who has spent ten years studying mathematics, five on dialectic, fifteen back in the cave performing military and administrative tasks, before finally studying the form of the good at the age of fifty. During the fifteen-year period in the cave, they are tested to see if they really can be trusted to hold power in the state (VII 539e3–540a2). All this seems to suggest that those who make it through to the end will not be liable to corruption of any kind.

In the *Phaedo*, however, Plato presents a different perspective. Here, true knowledge of the forms can only be achieved with the complete separation of the soul from the body, that is, at death. While still embodied, the philosopher's work is never complete: although he detaches himself as far as possible from the body, there will always be corporeal influences that impede his understanding (66d3–67b1). From this perspective, the philosopher never achieves perfection, as the *Republic* seems to suggest at VI 486e1–487a8.

---

[7] See Scott (2021).

[8] Or even inquiry situated lower down the divided line, in mathematics. See Section 2.1 with n. 3.

[9] See 486e1–487a8. At 486e2–3, he talks of soul that is going to have 'a sufficient and perfect apprehension of reality' (τῇ μελλούσῃ τοῦ ὄντος ἱκανῶς τε καὶ τελέως ψυχῇ μεταλήψεσθαι). He then talks of entrusting the state to people who 'are perfected (τελειωθεῖσι) by education and maturity of age' (487a7–8).

Perhaps the two dialogues just differ on this point. But there may be more convergence between them. In *Rep.* X 611b9–612a6, Socrates appears to take a perspective closer to the *Phaedo*, when he invokes the image of the sea-god Glaucus to describe the soul in its incarnate and discarnate states. While attached to the body it is 'maimed' (611b10–11). This could be taken to imply that, for any incarnate soul, bodily accretions (the senses and the non-rational desires) threaten to impede the work of reason. So, the *Republic* might differ from the *Phaedo* in allowing that philosophers can attain knowledge of forms even when incarnate (hence the references to perfection in VI 486e1–487a8). But this does not completely remove the risk of slippage: the verb 'maimed' (λελωβημένον, 611b10–11) is in the perfect tense, suggesting that the condition persists into the present. So, immersion in the world of particulars, that is, returning to the cave, might have deleterious effects on even the best characters, occluding their vision and even undermining their virtues. But this risk can be counteracted by long periods of contemplation outside the cave, which will sustain the philosopher's wisdom and keep the other virtues locked in place.

2.3 The Instrumental Value of Contemplation for the State

We can now turn to the civic value of contemplation. Because the question of intrinsic value will turn out to be more controversial in this context, I shall start with instrumental value. Here we can see how some of the points just made about the individual can easily be carried over to the state. This is obviously the case where the instrumental value of knowledge (*noēsis*) in practical decision-making is concerned. In fact, the point of introducing the forms in books V–VII is precisely to discuss something that will be useful – indeed indispensable – for the good running of the state (cf. 476a1–480a13, 484b4–d7, 520c3–d2 and 521b8–9).

Again, however, this is a point about the value of knowledge rather than contemplation. Are there grounds for saying contemplation itself is instrumentally good for the state? There are two. One follows directly on what we said earlier, about the way in which contemplation generates a string of moral qualities in the soul. This kind of instrumental value applies as much to the state as to the individual. In fact, Socrates discusses it primarily in a political context. At the beginning of book VI, he is still very much concerned to rebut the idea that philosophy and politics are incompatible with each other. So, in this passage, he is explicitly arguing that contemplation of forms generates a whole string of qualities required of a political leader. (Earlier, I was relying on the assumption that such qualities are also important in an individual's life.) Again, one might say that the contemplation here envisaged is only imperfect, not being based on full knowledge of the forms. But we can still say, as we did earlier, that contemplation in the strict sense might also have the role of helping to maintain the virtues of temperance, justice and the rest. To put it another way, when the philosophers are allowed a break from office and to leave cave for a period, they are refreshing their commitment to a worldview that helps lock their virtues in place, ready for when they return for their next period of rule.

So far, this is just to apply what we said about the instrumental value of contemplation for the individual to the state. But in book VII, Socrates argues in another way for the benefits of contemplation, which applies in the political context. At 519d4–521b11, he and Glaucon discuss the problem of the return to the cave. Philosophers who have left the cave will be reluctant to return from the 'the isles of the blest' (519c5) to the chores of ruling down in the cave, likened to Hades at 521c3. And yet they will return: as beneficiaries of the best education a state has to offer, they are bound by justice to rule when so required. But they will be only too happy to resume contemplation as soon as they are allowed.

In this passage, Socrates not only agrees with Glaucon that the philosophers view ruling in a negative light (they disdain it: 521b2); he goes as far as to capitalize on the fact: we need rulers like this, otherwise they will want to cling on to power and enter into competition with others, ultimately leading to faction within the state (521a4–8). And yet unity and cohesion are the most important political objectives (519e1–520a4). All this brings out a further instrumental benefit of contemplation. The mindset caused by the activity and experience of contemplation contributes to political unity. The very fact that philosophers have experienced the joys of contemplation further qualifies them to rule (over and above their ability to make the right decisions). They understand that, from the individual perspective, contemplation is an intrinsic good, the supreme good. This ensures that they approach power in the right way. In other words, the (perceived) intrinsic value of contemplation to the individual indirectly contributes to its instrumental value to the state.[10]

2.4 Contemplation as a Constituent of Civic *Eudaimonia*

We can now turn to the question of intrinsic value: is it just a good thing for the state that it includes people contemplating (in addition to the instrumental value

---

[10] That the philosophers disdain ruling cannot be in doubt (cf. 521b1–2: πολιτικῶν ἀρχῶν καταφρονοῦντα). At 540b3–4, Socrates is also clear that they see it as a chore and (surprisingly) not even as something fine (οὐχ ὡς καλόν τι). Beyond this, however, there is plenty of scholarly disagreement as to what their attitude implies. Are they really unwilling to rule (cf. 517c7–8) and does ruling involve a sacrifice of happiness on their part (cf. 520e4–521a2)? Brown (1998) 19 and Morrison (2001) 20 think that it does, while Irwin (1995) 313–16, Kraut (1999) 238 and Smith (2010) 91–98 take the other side. We do not need to resolve this dispute here. All is needed is the uncontroversial claim that philosophers, as a result of experiencing contemplation, will be keen to relinquish power when the opportunity arises.

that such contemplation brings)? To sharpen up the question, think again of the way Socrates allows the guardians to spend time contemplating when they are not ruling.[11] In such periods of leisure, are they continuing to benefit the state simply by contemplating? Or is the intrinsic benefit generated at this point merely for themselves, not for society?

Socrates never explicitly says in the *Republic* that philosophers add intrinsic value to the state just by the act of contemplation; he only ever mentions its instrumental value. But perhaps he endorses its intrinsic value to the state implicitly. One way of making the case for this comes from examining Plato's concept of civic *eudaimonia* more closely, and this will involve taking up the well-known debate between those who think Plato espoused an aggregative theory of civic happiness and those who opt for an organic one. Scholars who take the first approach think that for Plato the state's happiness consists in the happiness of a sufficient proportion of citizens. If correct, it implies that the happiness of philosophers who engage in contemplation will feed directly into the happiness of the state: although contemplation does have instrumental value, seen in this light it also constitutes a component of the civic good. Hence it has intrinsic value. The philosophers who have retreated to contemplate in the Elysian fields are still contributing to the general good.[12] If the aggregative interpretation were right, we would have found an implicit argument that contemplation is intrinsically good for the state.

In what follows, however, I shall claim that Plato endorsed a version of the organic theory: civic *eudaimonia* is a structural property of the state as a whole, sometimes characterised as harmony, but at certain points as unity. If so, contemplation will have only instrumental value, as something that helps maintain such unity. It is not a component of civic *eudaimonia*.

2.5 Plato's Organic Theory of Civic *Eudaimonia*

2.5.1 Preliminaries

The question of how Plato conceives of the happiness of the state in the *Republic* has proved notoriously controversial. According to Karl Popper in *The Open Society and its Enemies*, he espoused the 'organic' theory of the state and thought that individuals' happiness is entirely subordinate to the interests of this higher

---

[11] According to 520d9 and 540b1–2, the guardians spend most of their time contemplating. This is their default position, and they are called down to rule only when necessary.

[12] In this context, it is useful to bear in mind a distinction well-known to readers of the *NE*. Something can exist for the sake of *eudaimonia* in two different ways, either as an instrument for producing and maintaining it or as one of its components. In the latter case, it is both intrinsically good and 'for the sake of' *eudaimonia*. For discussion of this point in the *NE*, see Ackrill (1980) 19. For the application of the distinction to the *Republic*, see Irwin (1999) 167 and 174–78.

entity.[13] Subsequently, there was a fight-back, with some scholars, most notably Gregory Vlastos, accusing Popper of seriously misrepresenting Plato.[14] Instead, they argued, he espoused the view that civic happiness is merely the aggregate of individual happiness. But then a few scholars pushed back in the other direction, not all the way as far as Popper's polemic, but enough to claim that Plato did espouse some sort of organic theory, albeit one that is perhaps friendlier to individual happiness than Popper thought.[15]

When thinking about the organic theory in the context of Plato's *Republic*, it is important to distinguish between two elements of the theory.[16] First, there is a question about the state itself: is it an entity over and above its citizens, or merely an aggregate of them? Second, we can ask whether the happiness of the state is a property over and above the happiness of the individuals within it, or whether civic happiness is merely an aggregate of individual happiness. Plato has nothing explicit to say on the first question; the ontology of the state is distinctly under-theorised in the *Republic*. Where the second issue is concerned, there is more direct evidence to help us, even though happiness, especially civic happiness, does not receive the same explicit focus as the properties of justice, temperance, courage and wisdom in state and soul. In what follows, I shall concentrate on this second question; I do not think we need to establish a position about the first (the nature of the state) in order to answer it.

2.5.2 The Evidence of Book IV

The Statue Analogy

At the end of *Rep.* III, Socrates argues that the guardians will have no private property, living in austere conditions like soldiers on campaign (416d5–417b8). This prompts Adeimantus to object that, even though the city belongs to them, they enjoy no benefit from it (IV 419a1–420a2). Socrates replies that their task is not to make one particular group pre-eminently happy, but to make the city happy as a whole (420b5–8). To help his argument along, he compares the happiness of the city to the beauty of a statue (420c5–d5). Just because we thought the eyes were the supreme part of the statue, we would not paint them with the finest colour (purple); we would choose whatever colour contributes to the beauty of the whole (black). Similarly, we shall endow the guardians only with the resources to ensure that they

---

[13] The subordination of individual to state is a theme that runs throughout much of Popper's critique, but for specific references see Popper (1966) I 79–81 and 107–108, where he calls individuals 'cogs in the great clockwork of the state'.

[14] Vlastos (1995) 80–84. See also Levinson (1953) ch. 9, esp. 528–30, and Neu (1971).

[15] See esp. Morrison (2001), also Brown (1998) and Schofield (2006) 220–21.

[16] Morrison (2013) 186 discusses this distinction in relation to Aristotle's *Politics*.

best achieve the happiness of the whole city. To do otherwise would be to turn them into something other than guardians, just as eyes painted purple rather than black are no longer eyes (420d6–421b4).

Popper used this passage to show that Plato thought the state a distinct metaphysical entity, like a statue, which can have properties in its own right. What happens to the parts (be they the eyes of the statue or the citizens of the state) should be determined solely by whether it enhances the good of this super-entity.[17] In response, proponents of the opposing view, such as Gregory Vlastos, insisted that Plato is only contrasting the happiness of a few citizens with the greatest happiness of the greatest number, the point being that, if you bestow maximum happiness on one group, you do so at the expense of the aggregate happiness.[18]

In support of his view, Vlastos pointed out that this passage never contrasts the happiness of *all* the citizens with the happiness of the city as a whole, which is the contrast Popper needs; only the happiness of one group with that of the whole. Had Plato been making the former contrast, we would be forced to treat the happiness of the whole as something different from the aggregate, and the obvious way to do this would be to treat the happiness of the whole as an organic property. On its own, however, Vlastos' point shows only that the contrast Plato explicitly draws here cannot be used as evidence for the organic view. It does not actually establish the aggregate view, because it leaves unanswered the question of whether Plato is contrasting the happiness of select groups with the aggregate happiness or with the organic happiness of the state. So far, then, we have an open verdict.[19]

Vlastos on IV 420d6–e7

However, Vlastos has another trick up his sleeve, which involves getting into the nitty-gritty of the text immediately following the statue analogy. Consider this passage, where Socrates is responding to someone who presses Adeimantus' objection:

---

[17] Popper (1966) 107; see also Cross and Woozley (1964) 77–78 and 132.

[18] As well as Vlastos (1995) 80–84, see Neu (1971) 246 and Annas (1981) 179–80.

[19] It might be claimed that the very use of the statue analogy points towards the organic reading. To say that the beauty of an artwork is simply the aggregate of the beauty of all its parts would be an odd thesis to maintain. The beauty in question arises from the proportion or the structure among the parts. If we assumed this feature carries over in the analogy, we would have to adopt some sort of structural and hence organic account of civic *eudaimonia*. See Kraut (1999) 244–45. On the basis of this analogy, Morrison (2001) 14 talks of the happiness of the city as 'a gestalt property ... consisting in a pattern of relationships among the parts, rather than any kind of "sum" of their properties individually considered'. I think this a strong point but, in fairness to the other side, there is a question about how far we should push the analogy.

Don't require us to give the guardians the sort of happiness that would make them anything but guardians. For in the same way we could dress up the farmers in gorgeous robes and deck them with gold and tell them to work the land at their pleasure; and we could have the potters too recline in banquet-couches, left to right, boozing and feasting, with their potter's wheel alongside to potter with when they are so disposed; and all the others too we can make happy in the same fashion, so that indeed the whole city might be happy.[20]

Vlastos comments:

Here the happiness of the whole *polis* is not treated as something distinct from the happiness of the citizens; it is collapsed with theirs. The fact that the hypothesis is counterfactual – it would turn the *polis* into an amusement park, a 'country fair' (*hosper en panegurei* 421b2), and the result would be disastrous *un*happiness – in no way affects the point at issue, which is that *if* all the people in the *polis* could be made happy in this crazy way, then the whole *polis* would *be* happy.[21]

On this reading, Plato counter-factually assumes us making all these groups of people happy in the way described, but then inserts a premise that he himself believes to be true: that civic happiness is achieved by aggregating individual happiness. The result of this counter-factual would then indeed be civic happiness. Read this way, the last clause of the sentence, 'so that indeed the whole city might be happy' (ἵνα δὴ ὅλη ἡ πόλις εὐδαιμονῇ, 420e6–7), does show Plato endorsing the aggregate view.[22]

However, this relies on a misunderstanding of the Greek. Vlastos is treating these words as a consecutive clause: the result of our endowing all the citizens (individually) with happiness would be civic happiness. But in the Greek, the clause expresses purpose (the conjunction used is ἵνα not ὥστε): 'and all the others too we can make happy in the same fashion, *in order that* the whole city might be happy'. This dramatically changes things for anyone trying to decide between the organic and aggregative views of civic happiness: unlike the mistranslation that confuses a consecutive with a final clause, this translation does not pivot us either way. A correct paraphrase of the sentence (420d6–e7) would be: 'of course, in our attempt to make the whole city happy, we could treat all the citizens in the ways described, showering them with treats of various kinds.' Plato imagines us embarking on a doomed mission (as recommended by the objector) to spread happiness around the state by creating happiness in particular groups of individuals. This does not actually say anything about whether Plato's underlying conception of civic happiness is aggregative or organic; the point goes through either way. Those who hold the aggregative

---

[20] 420d6–e7. This translation is Vlastos' heavily modified version of Shorey (1937).
[21] Vlastos (1995) 82.   [22] Annas (1981) 179 agrees with Vlastos here.

view can say that the mission is doomed only because you will never make the individuals happy by allowing them to wine and dine; on the organic view, it is doomed both for this reason and because aggregating the happiness of individuals will not (necessarily) lead to happiness of the state. Read correctly, the passage does not imply an aggregative view of happiness.[23]

The Subsequent Argument (IV 420e7–421c5)

It is important to remember that the passage on which Vlastos' relies so heavily, 420d6–e7, constitutes only part of a larger argument. If we look at how the argument proceeds, can we find evidence for either view of civic happiness?

Immediately after 420d6–e7, Socrates claims that, if you follow the objector's advice and spoil the different groups in this way, 'a farmer won't be a farmer, or a potter a potter' (420e7–421a3). Indulgence causes them to lose their identity as craftsmen, and yet it is only through the existence of all these professions and crafts that the city comes into being. Next, he concedes that, if the cobblers (for instance) were corrupted and ceased to be cobblers, that would not have such a big impact on the city – presumably, it could still be happy even if its citizens were poorly shod. But it would be a disaster if the guardians were corrupted and ceased to be guardians, because the good management and happiness of the city depends on them. Indeed, if the guardians are no longer guardians, but merely revellers at a festival, the city will no longer be a city (421a4–b4). He concludes the argument as follows:

> We need to consider, then, whether we are to establish our guardians with this aim in view, to make them as happy as possible, or whether we should look to the city as a whole and consider if *it* is happy, and compel and persuade these auxiliaries and guardians of ours to do this, so that they'll be the best craftsmen at their own work, and all the others likewise. With the whole city prospering and well founded in this way, we should set aside the question of how nature assigns a share of happiness to each of the classes.[24]

Throughout this passage, 420e7–421c5, Socrates has been making two points: that their goal is not the happiness of a particular group, but of the whole city; and that they need to ensure that all the classes, especially the guardians, perform their functions. Of course, these two points are connected: the second

---

[23] Morrison (2001) 15, who argues for an organic view of civic happiness, seems to follow Vlastos in treating the ἵνα-clause as if it were a consecutive one, but he thinks the underlying premise – that you make the city happy by summing the happiness of the citizens – is held only by Socrates' opponents, not Socrates himself.

[24] 421b5–c5. This is my own translation. The way I render the last two lines ('we should set aside the question ... ') is controversial. Since it is important to my argument, I defend it in the appendix below (Section 2.8).

is a means towards achieving the first. In fact, it is the only means mentioned in the passage. At the end of the passage, he says that, once we have got everyone working away at their specific roles, the city will be well on course to achieve happiness (if not already happy). Then, strikingly, he sets aside the question of how each class (and hence each individual) can become happy.

All of this favours the organic reading. When thinking about the means for achieving the overall goal, he only mentions the need for each class to do its own work. On the organic reading, this is quite natural, because the crucial point is to ensure harmony and unity; and mutual, inter-related functioning is essential for achieving this. And the fact that, right at the end, he sets aside the question of individual happiness plays right into the hands of the organic theorist: civic happiness is a function of the structure of the city and the inter-relations of its constituent classes, not an amalgam of individual happiness. So we can leave questions about individual happiness to one side when considering how the state becomes happy.

By contrast, the aggregative reading struggles with this whole passage, especially the paragraph just quoted (421b5–c5). Of course, it does not deny the importance of each class performing its distinctive function as a means of ensuring civic happiness. But for the aggregative interpretation, that is only part of a wider account of how civic happiness is attained. There is a whole a causal chain to be considered: we compel people to stick to their tasks; this results in the city being well-ordered, but unless this leads to individuals being happy there can be no civic happiness, if such happiness is merely an aggregate of individual happiness. So we need to be sure how a city in which each class sticks to its role will result in individual happiness. Perhaps the idea is that, when someone performs their naturally given function, they derive some contentment or pleasure from it. Also, the results of having a well-ordered state, for example peace and stability, might give rise to individual happiness. But, either way, we need some such explanation to fill out the whole account and complete the causal chain. So why would Socrates be setting aside the question of how individuals become happy at the end? That would make no sense.

And even if we were to disregard the way he sets aside this question, there is still a problem for the aggregative view. It is striking that he makes no mention of any other means for achieving the goal of civic happiness than each class sticking to its function. But on the aggregative view, we need more than this – some explanation (such as I have just sketched) of how individual happiness results when each class sticks to its function. But where has he given this explanation? We could start scouring earlier books of the work to find an answer, but there is a strong objection to this strategy.

At V 465e5–466a6, he makes a back-reference to this passage and clearly implies that he had postponed the question of whether the guardians will attain happiness within the ideal state.[25] Only there does he attempt to answer this question. By his own admission, therefore, a crucial step in the aggregative view's understanding of the *Rep.* IV argument is missing until the following book.

2.5.3 Organic Unity in Books V and VII

There are two further passages relevant to understanding the nature of civic happiness, which can be found in books V and VII. Both favour a version of the organic reading. In V 457c10–466d4, Socrates argues that they need to avoid having nuclear families among the guardians and auxiliaries in order to prevent conflict from breaking out in the city. Instead, the city will be bound together when everyone addresses their fellow citizens in familial terms: 'brother' or 'sister' for people of a similar age, 'mother' or 'father' for the generation above, and 'son' or 'daughter' for the generation below.[26] Obviously, the abolition of the family is an extreme measure, but Socrates justifies it by stressing the need to avoid dissension in the city:

> 'Is not the logical first step towards such an agreement to ask ourselves what we could name as the greatest good for the constitution of a state and the proper aim of a lawgiver in his legislation, and what would be the greatest evil, and then to consider whether the proposals we have just set forth fit into the footprints of the good and do not suit those of the evil?' 'By all means,' he said. 'Do we know of any greater evil for a state than the thing that tears it apart and makes it many instead of one, or a greater good than that which binds it together and makes it one?' 'We do not.' (462a2–b3)

What he is doing here is stating the overall goal (the 'proper aim') at which the lawgiver aims, the *summum bonum* of the state.[27] And it turns out that this goal is unity. Although this does not show conclusively that Plato has turned the state into a super-entity, it does show that the ultimate goal has become the promotion of an organic property, not an aggregate one.[28]

Further evidence for the organic interpretation comes from book VII, in the discussion about compelling the philosophers to return to the cave (519d4–521b11). Glaucon has just protested that, by expecting the philosophers to rule, we are making them live a worse life than they would if they stayed in the 'isles of the

---

[25] I discuss this back-reference further in Section 2.8.

[26] Initially the point applies to the guardians (463c1–5) but it is generalised to all citizens at 463d6.

[27] That Plato is talking about the final good of the state is clear from his language here: τὸ μέγιστον ἀγαθὸν ... οὗ δεῖ στοχαζόμενον τὸν νομοθέτην τιθέναι τοὺς νόμους (462a3–5).

[28] For a discussion of the stress on unity in V 462a2–b3, see Schofield (2006) 214–15, also Scott (2008) 370–372.

blest', the world outside the cave. Socrates then reminds him that their task is not to make one group pre-eminently happy:

> 'You have again forgotten, my friend,' I said, 'that the law is not concerned to make one class in the state do particularly well, but is trying to produce this condition in the city as a whole, harmonizing and adapting the citizens to one another by persuasion and compulsion, and requiring them to impart to one another any benefit which they are severally able to bestow upon the community, and that it itself creates such men in the state, not that it may allow each to take what course pleases him, but with a view to using them for binding the city together.' (519e1–520a4)

Here, Socrates is reminding Glaucon of the discussion he had with Adeimantus at the beginning of book IV, about whether we should aim at the happiness of the guardians in particular. Before we turn to the significance of this, we should just underline the point he is making in this passage. The law is focused not on the happiness of a particular group, but on unifying the city together – the same point made about the lawmaker in V 462a2–b3. He does not say that our concern is also with making particular groups happy; it is simply binding the citizens together that he singles out as the goal.

The fact that he links this to the discussion at the beginning of book IV (cf. 519e1–3 with 420b5–8) is very important from our point of view. It means we are entitled to read each passage in the light of the other. Using book IV to fill out VII 519e1–520a4, we can say that the goal being aimed at is civic happiness – the happiness of the city as a whole.[29] Using book VII to fill out the text in book IV, we can infer that the happiness referred to there (e.g. at 420b7–8) consists in some sort of binding together, or unity (to bring V 462a2–b3 into the picture). The book IV passage merely said (somewhat vaguely) that our aim is the happiness of the city as a whole; in the light of the book VII text, we can describe the goal more specifically: to do everything they can to bind the city together as a whole (ἐπὶ τὸν σύνδεσμον τῆς πόλεως, 520a3–4).[30] So the import of the book VII passage is that you create the ultimate good, civic *eudaimonia*, not by aggregating the good of the parts within it, but by so ordering them that you create a unity out of the whole.[31] This helps to confirm our organic reading of IV 420b3–421c5.

---

[29] In VII 519e2, Socrates uses the expression 'doing well' (*eu prattein*) rather than 'happiness' (*eudaimonia*). But he must have happiness in mind, given the link with book IV. For the closeness of 'doing well' and 'happiness', see I 353e4–354a2.

[30] Brown (1998) 22 also uses this text as evidence for an organic strand in Plato's theory and rightly castigates Vlastos (1995) 82–84 for using a truncated translation of the passage to defend the aggregative reading.

[31] This connection between oneness and goodness is, of course, something that Plato is said to have espoused outside the work in his notorious lecture on the Good. See Aristoxenus, *Elementa Harmonica* II 30–31, translated in Barnes (1984) II 2397.

2.5.4 Contemplation and Organic Eudaimonia

We can now return to our overall question about the civic value of contempla-tion. Having ruled out the aggregative view of civic happiness, we can block one route that might be taken to say that, merely by contemplating and without actually ruling, the philosophers contribute intrinsic value to the state.

On its own, this point leaves open the possibility that Plato had other reasons for attaching intrinsic value to contemplation, for the state as well as the individual. But we could draw a stronger conclusion and use our account of civic happiness to rule out this possibility without further ado. As well as arguing that civic happiness is an organic property, we have also identified it with proportion, harmony and unity, and this has implications for the kind of value contemplation can have in a political context. If civic happiness just is proportion, harmony and unity, how can mere contemplation be intrinsically good for the state? For the reasons given in Section 2.3, it will help promote such happiness instrumentally. But contemplation is not a component of the *summum bonum*; it is not, from the point of view of the state, an intrinsic good that can be set alongside other such goods and viewed as a part of the overall good. Hence it should be no surprise that Plato nowhere talks of contemplation as intrinsically good for the state; he does not think that it is.

Before endorsing this stronger conclusion, however, I wish to consider one further argument for making contemplation intrinsically valuable to the state. This stems from considering the civic virtue of wisdom (*sophia*), which Socrates describes in his account of the state's virtues in *Rep.* IV.

2.6 *Sophia* in Book IV

When Glaucon introduces the distinction between intrinsic and instrumental goods at the beginning of book II, he uses knowing as an example of something that counts as good in both ways (357c3).[32] Given the context (he is speaking intuitively), he is most likely thinking of what is good for an individual. But suppose we could make sense of the idea that the state, as such, can exercise knowledge. After all, a state is often spoken of as engaging in other kinds of activity – declaring war, making peace, conducting negotiations, and generally enacting decisions; so why cannot it be said to exercise knowledge? If it can, we might assume, on Plato's behalf, that the same point made about the individual in II 357c3 applies to the state: exercising knowledge is intrinsically as well as instrumentally good for it.

---

[32] I take τὸ φρονεῖν here to refer to the act of knowing, though some translate it as a mere state (of knowledge, wisdom or intelligence): see Ferrari and Griffith (2000), Grube (1974), Lee (1974) and Waterfield (1993).

Now, at IV 427e9 and 428b4–429a3, Socrates claims that the state, as such, can be wise. If it has the virtue of wisdom (*sophia*), then, in exercising it on specific occasions, it presumably exercises knowledge. Following the logic of Glaucon's claim about the individual in II 357c3, we can say that, in exercising such wisdom or knowledge, it achieves something intrinsically good for itself (as well as deriving instrumental benefit).

In outline, this is true. One point in favour of the proposal is that wisdom really is a virtue of the state, not merely of individuals within it. This point is easily overlooked. When discussing the state's temperance at IV 431e10–432a3, Socrates contrasts it with wisdom and courage: while those virtues can be traced back to a particular class in the state (the guardians and auxiliaries respectively), temperance is spread across the whole (likewise justice). However, this contrast is not made in order to reduce wisdom to the possession of wisdom among the guardians (or to reduce the courage of the state to individual courage among the auxiliaries). Look at the way he describes wisdom in the state in book IV:

> Then it is by virtue of its smallest class and minutest part of itself, and the wisdom that resides therein, in the part which takes the lead and rules, that a city established on principles of nature would be wise as a whole. (428e7–9)

Civic wisdom is a complex package, involving at least three elements. The first will be the possession of *noēsis* by individual guardians.[33] The second is the application of that knowledge to particulars. Shortly before the text I have quoted, Socrates says that wisdom deliberates 'about the city as a whole and the betterment of its relations with itself and other states' (428d2–3). Of course, Plato ultimately thinks that such deliberations require knowledge of the forms, the same knowledge at issue in the activity of contemplation; but what is being held up here and defined as wisdom is a cognitive state that marries knowledge of forms with a grasp of particular facts, issuing in practical guidance.

The third element concerns the effectiveness of the citizens who possess wisdom in their souls. A city with a group of people who possess knowledge of forms and know how to apply it to practical decisions, but who have no political power, is not a wise state. Otherwise, any city that happened to include philosophers who spring up spontaneously (cf. 520b3, *automatoi*) would be wise. It is crucial that the group of people who possess wisdom individually is described as 'the part which takes the lead and rules' (428e8). To assert that a state is wise presupposes that the practical insights of the guardians are

---

[33] I am assuming that *sophia* involves knowledge of forms, *noēsis*. This assumption, of course, involves reading books V–VII into book IV.

accepted and followed by the other two classes. The same point recurs when he applies the definition to wisdom in the soul:

> But wise by that small part *that ruled in him* and handed down these commands, by its possession in turn within it of the knowledge of what is beneficial for each and for the whole, the community composed of the three. (442c4–7, emphasis added)

This is what I meant by saying that civic wisdom is a complex package. Only once all these three elements are combined – knowledge of forms (*noēsis*), the application of that knowledge (through perception) to particulars, and the power to enact it – do we find civic wisdom. And now it should be clear that this virtue is genuinely corporate, not reducible to the wisdom of a few citizens, but a property of the whole entity.[34]

If civic wisdom is a *bona fide* corporate virtue, there can be corporate knowing (*phronein*). But it does not follow that the mere contemplation exercised by the philosophers in the ideal state is a case of corporate knowing, because we have just seen that civic wisdom is more than the knowledge exercised in contemplation (*noēsis*). This means that the actualisation of civic wisdom is not the same as contemplation, which is a simpler kind of knowing. Hence, even if we take the actualisation of wisdom as a case of corporate knowing, we have no licence to say that mere contemplation, as exercised by the guardians in their periods outside the cave, counts as a corporate activity (And our attempt to apply Glaucon's example of knowing in II 357c3 as an intrinsic good for the state depended on locating a genuinely corporate form of knowing.) If so, we cannot claim that contemplation has intrinsic value for the state; we have not shown that the state is the agent of such knowing.

So far, this seems to confirm only the weaker conclusion drawn earlier – that Plato does not explicitly make contemplation intrinsically good for the state. But what about the stronger conclusion – that, given the identification of civic happiness with harmony and unity, contemplation can only ever have instrumental value? What we have just said about wisdom complicates the picture. On my view, civic happiness is exhausted by unity and harmony; and yet the exercise of wisdom, which appears to be something different from unity and harmony, has intrinsic value. The implication of this is that for Plato something can be intrinsically good for the state even without being a component of *eudaimonia*. If so, we cannot

---

[34] One might wonder whether this blurs the boundary between wisdom and justice: the former seems to require the latter, in so far as it needs all classes in the state to perform their own functions and not interfere with each other. But we should welcome this point, because at 433b8–9 Socrates says that justice enables the other virtues to come into being.

mount the stronger argument that anything not included in the ambit of *eudaimonia* can only have instrumental value.

Nonetheless, I think the stronger conclusion still stands. This is because civic wisdom cannot so easily be divorced from unity and harmony. We have analysed it as a 'gestalt' property, which involves the appropriate and harmonious relations between the different classes in the state. It is not mere understanding; it is in fact one manifestation of the harmony and unity in which the state's *eudaimonia* consists, because it involves different parts of the state being bonded together under the supervision of the guardians' expertise. This means that gestalt properties like unity and harmony can still be seen to exhaust the content of civic happiness.

2.7 Conclusion

One implication of my view is that there is an asymmetry between Plato's approaches to individual and to civic happiness: contemplation is a component of the former, but only a means to the latter. Is this consistent with the state-soul parallel? Here, he makes the unitarian assumption that, when we use a term to apply to two things (e.g. 'just' to both state and soul), it has the same sense in both cases (IV 435a6–9). Socrates adheres to this principle when analysing the four virtues of state and soul (IV 441c4–444c4); should we not expect him to do the same for *eudaimonia*? In other words, if *eudaimonia* for the state consists in unity and harmony, the same should apply to the soul; and if contemplation only has value as a means to that harmony when it comes to the state, the same ought to apply to the soul – contrary to my interpretation.

However, Socrates does not apply anything like the same attention to the analysis of *eudaimonia* in the *Republic* as he does to the virtues. In my view, his approach to individual *eudaimonia* develops as the work progresses, and this is because his views on the nature of the soul start to change. Up to the end of book IV, it is quite possible that individual *eudaimonia* tracks civic *eudaimonia* quite closely: unity and harmony do seem uppermost in Socrates' mind when he talks about how justice benefits the individual soul and promotes its happiness at IV 443d5–e2. But he might have changed his position on the nature of the soul after he has introduced the metaphysics of the central books. The best evidence for this comes towards the end of the work, at X 611d8–612a6.[35] Socrates has just argued for the immortality of the soul and now raises the possibility that the soul's true nature is not tripartite but consists entirely of reason (the only element in us that survives the death of the body, unlike appetite and spirit). For us, the importance of this point is that, if the soul is not tripartite, it can no

---

[35] I mentioned this passage in Section 2.2.

longer be parallel to the state with its three classes of guardians, auxiliaries and producers. Admittedly, this passage only suggests that the soul might not be tripartite. But, at the very least, it leaves the question of the soul's true nature open for further investigation.[36] And, as long as there is a question mark over this issue, it is no longer clear how similar the *eudaimonia* of the (true) soul will be to that of the tripartite state.[37]

2.8 Appendix: The Translation of *Rep*. IV 421c3–5

Towards the end of Section 2.5.2, I discussed the significance of the way Socrates concludes his response to Adeimantus' objection at the beginning of book IV. I translated the final few lines of Socrates' response as follows:

> We need to consider, then, whether we are to establish our guardians with this aim in view, to make them as happy as possible, or whether we should look to the city as a whole and consider if *it* is happy, and compel and persuade these auxiliaries and guardians of ours to do this, so that they'll be the best craftsmen at their own work, and all the others likewise. With the whole city prospering and well founded in this way, we should set aside the question of how nature assigns a share of happiness to each of the classes. (421b5–c5)

> σκεπτέον οὖν πότερον πρὸς τοῦτο βλέποντες τοὺς φύλακας καθιστῶμεν, ὅπως ὅτι πλείστη αὐτοῖς εὐδαιμονία ἐγγενήσεται, ἢ τοῦτο μὲν εἰς τὴν πόλιν ὅλην βλέποντας θεατέον εἰ ἐκείνη ἐγγίγνεται, τοὺς δ' ἐπικούρους τούτους καὶ τοὺς φύλακας ἐκεῖνο ἀναγκαστέον ποιεῖν καὶ πειστέον, ὅπως ὅτι ἄριστοι δημιουργοὶ τοῦ ἑαυτῶν ἔργου ἔσονται, καὶ τοὺς ἄλλους ἅπαντας ὡσαύτως, καὶ οὕτω συμπάσης τῆς πόλεως αὐξανομένης καὶ καλῶς οἰκιζομένης ἐατέον ὅπως ἑκάστοις τοῖς ἔθνεσιν ἡ φύσις ἀποδίδωσι τοῦ μεταλαμβάνειν εὐδαιμονίας.

Although most of my translation is uncontroversial, I depart from other English versions in the way I render the end of the sentence: 'we should set aside the question of how nature assigns a share of happiness to each of the classes'. Grube is representative of the more usual approach: 'we must leave it to nature to provide each group with its share of happiness'.[38]

The difference between my translation and the orthodox one is important in the debate over how Plato conceived of civic happiness. As I pointed out in

---

[36] For further discussions of this passage, see Robinson (1967), Szlezák (1976) and Woolf (2012).

[37] In other words, where the property of *eudaimonia* is concerned, the unitarian assumption can be questioned. In Scott (2015) 17–18, I argued that this assumption is just a provisional hypothesis in any case.

[38] Grube (1997). All the English translations and commentaries that I have consulted conform to this way of understanding the text. It also appears in Cousin (1833), Schmelzer (1884), Apelt (1916), Baccou (1936), Chambry (1959) and Rufener and Szlezák (2003), all *ad loc*. See also Arends (1988) 131. The only exception I have found Schleiermacher (1828), as I discuss in n. 44.

Section 2.5.2, my version makes him set aside the question of how nature enables the citizens of the ideal state to enjoy happiness as individuals. For the reasons I gave earlier, this strongly favours the organic view. By contrast, the standard translation appears compatible with both the organic and aggregative theories of civic happiness. (1) Advocates of the organic view will say that the happiness of the city is reached as soon as it is 'well ordered' (καλῶς οἰκιζομένης, 421c3). The rest of the sentence refers to something that is not part and parcel of civic happiness: the happiness of individual classes (and hence citizens). So, on the standard translation, once the city is well-ordered and happy, our job is done, and we leave it to nature to sort out individual happiness as something that lies outside our aim as founders. (2) For advocates of the aggregative view, the last clause constitutes an important stage in the process of securing civic happiness: the process started with individual classes sticking to their tasks; that led to the city becoming well-ordered; nature will then see to it that individual classes get what happiness they can; then, in the final stage (not actually stated), once individuals have attained their happiness, this can all be aggregated so that we have achieved civic happiness.

So the standard translation leaves both interpretations in the running; my translation does not. In the light of this, it is important to establish which is correct. The difficult lies solely with the last clause: ἐατέον ὅπως ἑκάστοις τοῖς ἔθνεσιν ἡ φύσις ἀποδίδωσι τοῦ μεταλαμβάνειν εὐδαιμονίας (421c3–5). First, we need to look into the meaning of the word ἐατέον. This is a verbal adjective, derived from ἐάω. Aside from the occurrence of the word in our passage, there are twenty-two uses of it elsewhere in Plato and they fall neatly into two categories. Sometimes it means 'one should allow' in the sense of granting permission. In *Rep.* II–III there is a cluster of such uses in the section dealing with the censorship of poetry, where Socrates discusses what sort of content should be allowed in the ideal state.[39] The second sense of ἐατέον is 'one should dismiss'; occasionally the term is coupled with χαίρειν, 'one should say good-bye to'.[40] Some of these uses concern a context in which we are being told to dismiss (or, at least, leave on one side) an issue, problem or question.[41] Excluding the use of the term in our passage, ἐατέον appears twelve times meaning 'dismiss' or 'abandon'; ten times meaning 'permit' or 'allow'.

Now turn to in the remainder of the sentence: ὅπως ἑκάστοις τοῖς ἔθνεσιν ἡ φύσις ἀποδίδωσι τοῦ μεταλαμβάνειν εὐδαιμονίας. What sort of clause does ὅπως introduce? The conjunction can introduce a final clause (and other related kinds of clause, expressing aim or aspiration); it can also introduce a relative

---

[39] 380a2 and 7, b3 and 5; 390d7. Cf. 401b7.   [40] *Statesman* 260b11 and *Laws* 832e3.
[41] *Philebus* 20a6, *Phaedrus* 239d8, *Laws* 822c8 and 965e6.

clause or an indirect question. If it is a final clause it has to be followed by a future indicative or a subjunctive. But here it is followed by a present indicative. So it cannot be expressing an aim or intention; it either introduces a relative clause expressing the manner in which nature distributes happiness to individual groups in the city, or an indirect question – the question of how nature distributes such happiness.

We can now put the two pieces together. The ὅπως-clause follows directly after ἐατέον. I can make no sense of this juxtaposition if ἐατέον means 'we must permit': what follows is either an indirect question or a relative clause, but 'we must permit how nature distributes happiness' sounds bizarre. Those who adopt this sense of ἐατέον are in effect reading the text as if Plato had said that we must allow nature to distribute happiness. But if ἐατέον meant this, ἡ φύσις would have to be an accusative as the direct object of ἐατέον, and ἀποδίδωσι an infinitive: 'we should allow nature to distribute . . . '. The standard translation is not actually a translation of the Greek that we have before us.[42]

Instead, let us try the other sense of ἐατέον: 'we should dismiss'. If ὅπως introduces an indirect question (which is more likely than a relative clause), this reading seems far more plausible on purely philological grounds. It makes obvious sense to talk of dismissing, or putting to one side, a question. As I said in footnote 41, some uses of ἐατέον appear in just this context. Hence my proposed translation: 'we should set aside the question of how nature assigns a share of happiness to each of the classes.' There is a grammatical parallel to this within the *Republic* itself. Plato uses the verb ἐάω with an indirect question at VI 506d7–8: αὐτὸ μὲν τί ποτ' ἐστὶ τἀγαθὸν ἐάσωμεν τὸ νῦν εἶναι ('let's leave on one side what the good itself is for the time-being').[43] The verbal adjective ἐατέον can also be found with an indirect question in the pseudo-Aristotelian work, *On Melissus, Xenophanes, and Gorgias* 975a19:

---

[42] As Adam (1963) I 209, following Jowett and Campbell (1894) III 165, effectively admits; cf. also Emlyn-Jones and Preddy (2013) I 347 n. 6.

[43] One could challenge the closeness of my parallel between 506d7–8 and 421c3–5. On my reading ἐατέον is followed immediately by an indirect question, without any direct object. (The other uses of ἐατέον cited in n. 41, where it means setting aside an issue, take an object in the accusative.) However, one could argue that in 506d7–8 Plato inserts a direct object between ἐάσωμεν and the question, αὐτὸ μὲν τἀγαθὸν being the direct object of ἐάσωμεν, and τί ποτ' ἐστὶ specifying something about it: 'we shall leave aside the good itself, i.e. what it is'. If so, this would not be the close parallel that I have claimed. But my understanding of the text is that the function of the αὐτὸ is to specify that we are leaving aside the good *itself*, in contrast to its *offspring* (ἔκγονός, e2), which forms the other half of the μὲν . . . δὲ contrast. Thus, ἐάσωμεν goes directly with the question τί ποτ' ἐστὶ τἀγαθόν; αὐτὸ μὲν is separated from τἀγαθὸν and put first for emphasis, making the contrast with ἔκγονός clear. Notice also that there is another use of ἐᾶν at the end of this text (e3): ὃς δὲ ἔκγονός τε τοῦ ἀγαθοῦ φαίνεται καὶ ὁμοιότατος ἐκείνῳ, λέγειν ἐθέλω, εἰ καὶ ὑμῖν φίλον, εἰ δὲ μή, ἐᾶν. Presumably the ellipsis at the end needs to be filled out as: ὃς δὲ ἔκγονός τε τοῦ ἀγαθοῦ φαίνεται καὶ ὁμοιότατος ἐκείνῳ, ἐᾶν ἐθέλω. If so, that is another case of ἐᾶν meaning 'leave aside' followed directly by a clause, without a direct object mediating it. (Grammatically, ἐᾶν functions like λέγειν in e3.)

Ἀλλ' ἆρα εἰ μὲν δυνατά ἐστιν ἢ ἀδύνατα ἃ λέγει, ἐατέον ('But we should aside whether what he says is possible or impossible'). This is how we should take the grammar of *Rep.* 421c3–5. As such, the Greek is completely natural.[44]

There is an interesting postscript to all this. In book V, towards the end of the discussion of the second wave of paradox, Socrates talks of the benefits that the guardians and auxiliaries will derive from being in the city. The harmony and fellow feeling that he has discussed mean that they enjoy security; all the necessities of life are provided for (without the stress that wealthy people have in managing their property). They will be even more fortunate than Olympic victors, who traditionally enjoyed not only honour, but also free meals for life at the state's expense. At this point, having waxed so lyrical about the life of the guardians, he recalls their discussion from the beginning of book IV:

> Do you recall … that in the preceding argument the objection of somebody or other rebuked us for not making our guardians happy, since, though it was in their power to have everything that belongs to the citizens, they had nothing, and we, I believe, replied that this was a consideration to which we would return if occasion offered, but that at present we were making our guardians into guardians and the city as a whole as happy as possible, and that we were not modelling our ideal of happiness with reference to any one class? (465e5–466a6)

> Μέμνησαι οὖν, ἦν δ' ἐγώ, ὅτι ἐν τοῖς πρόσθεν οὐκ οἶδα ὅτου λόγος ἡμῖν ἐπέπληξεν ὅτι τοὺς φύλακας οὐκ εὐδαίμονας ποιοῦμεν, οἷς ἐξὸν πάντα ἔχειν τὰ τῶν πολιτῶν οὐδὲν ἔχοιεν; ἡμεῖς δέ που εἴπομεν ὅτι τοῦτο μέν, εἴ που παραπίπτοι, εἰς αὖθις σκεψόμεθα, νῦν δὲ τοὺς μὲν φύλακας φύλακας ποιοῦμεν, τὴν δὲ πόλιν ὡς οἷοί τ' εἶμεν εὐδαιμονεστάτην, ἀλλ' οὐκ εἰς ἓν ἔθνος ἀποβλέποντες ἐν αὐτῇ τοῦτο εὔδαιμον πλάττοιμεν.

Socrates is clearly referring to Adeimantus' challenge at the beginning of book and to his reply (419a1–421c5). But there is an enigma here: he says they promised to return to the issue of the guardians' happiness if the occasion permitted. Where did they make this promise?

I do not think he ever made such a promise explicitly. But our translation of 421c3–5 offers some help. There, Socrates says that they should leave on one side the question of how nature apportions the different classes a share in happiness, the very question he answers in 465e5–466a6, at least for the case of the guardians and auxiliaries. At 421c3–5, he did not say whether he was leaving the question on one side permanently, that is, dismissing it, or whether

---

[44] I was feeling a little insecure in taking issue with just about every translation of 421c3–5 I had come across. But then I was relieved to find myself in the august company of Schleiermacher (1828): 'Also müssen wir doch erwägen, … ob wir nicht, wenn nur der ganze Staat gedeiht und gut eingerichtet ist, es schon gehen lassen sollen, wie für jede einzelne Abteilung die Natur es mit sich bringt an der gemeinen Glückseligkeit Teil zu nehmen.' See also Schleiermacher and Chambry (1971).

he was just temporarily postponing it.[45] If I am right in my translation of 421c3–5, we have a partial solution: when he says in book V that they promised to return to the issue (if the occasion arose), he at least implies that they earlier put it to one side. This dovetails with my reading of 421c3–5.[46] By contrast, the standard translation renders the back-reference in book V a complete enigma.

All this confirms a point that some commentators have made against Popper's critique of the *Republic*:[47] Plato is not indifferent to the happiness of particular groups (especially not the guardians, which was the point of Adeimantus' complaint). If he were, he would presumably have dismissed the question of their happiness permanently. Perhaps we can say that, although the happiness of the state is an organic, structural property, Plato still expects us to be concerned with individual happiness. There is a distinction between what constitutes civic happiness and what our concerns as founders are. As founders we are concerned to promote civic happiness, an organic property, but also to be aware of the individual happiness of our citizens.[48]

3 Aristotle on the Social Value of Contemplation

3.1 Introduction

We now turn to Aristotle's views on the civic value of contemplation, specifically the question of how contemplation contributes towards civic happiness in the ideal state. As in my discussion of Plato, I shall approach this topic by tackling the broader issue of how Aristotle conceives of civic happiness, whether he sees it as an aggregative or an organic property. Once this is answered, we can explain how the contemplative activity of certain individuals within the state contributes to its overall happiness.[49]

---

[45] In the grammatically parallel passage at VI 506d7–8, they left a question aside 'for the present' (τὸ νῦν εἶναι).

[46] It is interesting that Plato inserts the particle που when he makes the back-reference at 466a3 (ἡμεῖς δέ που εἴπομεν ὅτι τοῦτο μέν ...). This word can signify uncertainty: see Denniston (1981) 490–91. Hence some translations insert 'I think' (or the like) into the back-reference: as quoted above, Shorey (1937) inserts 'I believe', as does Sachs (2007). Grube (1997) has 'I think', and Ferrari and Griffith (2000) insert 'if I remember rightly'. This would further ease the sense of mystery – Plato is being deliberately approximate in his back-reference. The same particle occurs in two other back-references in the *Republic*: 504b1 and 588b2. In the first case, scholars have also noted (and worried about) a slight mismatch between the earlier and later passages. I discuss this apparent mismatch in Scott (2015) 44–45.

[47] E.g. Levinson (1953) 528–29 and Neu (1971) 244–49.

[48] When describing the virtue of wisdom in the individual, Socrates says it involves 'knowledge of what is beneficial for each and for the whole, the community composed of the three' (IV 442c5–7). Assuming this also applies to civic wisdom, we can be confident that the founders will be concerned with individual as well as civic happiness.

[49] One might wonder how far the ideal states of the *Republic* and the *Politics* are comparable. Aristotle is obviously interested in the ideal state in its own right and is talking about a city that he thinks might come into being. By contrast, the ideally just state of the *Republic* is introduced as

By way of an introduction, I shall briefly set out the texts that we shall be consulting (in this Section and in Section 4), along the way giving an outline of the nature of Aristotelian contemplation.[50] As before, I shall also use this introduction to describe the kind of value that contemplating has for the individual. This will help us answer our main question about its value for the state.

3.1.1 The Relevant Texts

The *Nicomachean Ethics* (NE)

Our primary focus will be on passages in the *NE* and the *Politics* that discuss the value of contemplation and the nature of civic happiness. Within the *NE*, the best-known discussion of contemplation comes in X 7–8, but we should start with material relevant to its nature in book VI, which discusses the different intellectual virtues, operating with a broad distinction between practical and theoretical reason. The former is involved in the life of moral and political activity, the latter in the life of contemplation. In *NE* VI 1, 1038b35–1039a17, Aristotle argues that this distinction has a psychological dimension, in that the two kinds of reason belong to different parts of the soul (a point repeated in X 7, 1177b27–9 and 8, 1178a16–22). There is also a metaphysical basis to the distinction: theoretical reason is concerned with what is unchanging, eternal and necessary (VI 3, 1139b19–24). This leads him to include scientific and philosophical activity within the realm of contemplation, and to exclude practical thinking about human affairs, which is the concern of a different intellectual virtue, *phronēsis* (VI 12, 1143b19–20).

When it comes to outlining the virtues of the theoretical intellect, book VI divides them into three: *epistēmē* (VI 3), *nous* (VI 3) and *sophia* (VI 7).[51] *Epistēmē* involves proof, understanding how the propositions of a science follow from its first principles. *Nous* is knowledge of those first principles: since they are axiomatic, they cannot be derived by way of proof and therefore

---

a heuristic device to elucidate justice in the individual (II 368c8–369b3). Furthermore, it is a matter of debate as to whether Socrates thinks it could ever become as reality. Nonetheless, we should not exaggerate the differences. As the *Republic* goes on, the interlocutors become interested in the account of the ideal state as a project in its own right: how else to explain the sheer amount of detail invested in the description of its rulers and their education, for instance? As for the question of whether Socrates thought the ideal state realisable, my own view is that he does, as is suggested by VI 499c1–d7 and 502a5–c8. However, it would take us too far afield to discuss this in a detail. For a recent discussion, see Vegetti (2013).

[50] For the purposes of this Section, we only need an outline. When we turn to the question of how widely contemplation extends among the citizenry in Section 4, we shall go into more detail, especially about the kinds of disciplines that might fall under the term, for example, natural sciences, mathematics and theology.

[51] Translators vary widely in the way they render these words, and it will be more helpful just to stay with the original terms. For an overview of Aristotle's epistemology and the difference between these kinds of intellectual virtue, see Taylor (1990).

cannot be the object of *epistēmē*.[52] *Sophia* is the state that combines knowledge of principles and proofs.

While *NE* VI says little about the relative value of contemplation and moral or political activity, the topic comes to the fore in book X.[53] In X 6–8, Aristotle proposes to give an outline account of *eudaimonia*, now that he has discussed virtue, friendship and pleasure. He starts by rejecting the life of amusement as a candidate for *eudaimonia* in X 6, before turning to the relative claims of intellectual contemplation and moral-cum-political activity in chapters 7–8.

X 7 consists of a string of arguments in favour of taking contemplation to constitute perfect *eudaimonia*. The first is that *eudaimonia* is activity in accordance with the highest virtue of which we are capable, that is, theoretical intellect, and which is in some sense divine; hence perfect *eudaimonia* will be intellectual contemplation (1177a12–18). He then advances five additional arguments, before returning to the divinity of contemplation at the end of the chapter and defending himself against the objection that, as mere mortals, we should not be attempting to lead the life of the gods. On the contrary, he replies, we should pursue this aspect of our nature as far as we can (1177b33–4).

If contemplation has such exalted status, what value should we attach to the life of moral virtue? In answer to this, X 8 argues that it is 'happiest in a secondary way' (1178a9). I take this to mean that such a life constitutes not perfect, but a second-best form of happiness.[54] The chapter then discusses the difference between the practical and contemplative lives, as well as offering us reasons for valuing the practical, even though contemplation is superior. Finally, returning to the spirit of X 7, he ends with two more arguments in favour of the superiority of the contemplative life by comparing it to that of the gods (1178b7–32 and 1179a22–32).

The *Politics*

Although the account of contemplation in *NE* X is very well-known, the topic also features in *Pol.* VII as part of its discussion of the ideal state. As in *NE* X, some of this focuses on the comparison between the contemplative and political lives.

Pol. VII opens with the claim that, to understand what the best or ideal state is like, we need to identify the most choiceworthy life (VII 1, 1323a14–16). Aristotle also raises the question of whether the life that is most choiceworthy for the state is the same as for the individual (1323a21–2). This he answers in the affirmative right at the beginning of the following chapter (1324a5–13).

---

[52] As Aristotle says at VI 3, 1139b27, his conception of *epistēmē* is explained in the *Analytics* (specifically the *Posterior Analytics* I 1–6; on *nous*, see II 19).

[53] Aristotle does link divinity to contemplation in VI 7, 1141a20–22, b1–3 and 7. See Section 4.4.1.

[54] I have discussed this in Scott (1999).

Having asserted the need to identify the most choiceworthy life, he spends three chapters considering some candidates. Chapter 1 is a debate between two positions about the importance of virtue in the best life. He distinguishes three kinds of good: external (e.g. wealth, power and reputation), bodily (e.g. health) and internal goods of the soul (the virtues); then he asks which goods have priority (1323a24–35). On one view, the goal is to maximise external goods and only to pursue virtue in so far as it helps us acquire them. But Aristotle proceeds to argue for the reverse position: that virtue has priority, and that we should pursue externals only up to a limit, that is, in so far as they aid us in pursing the virtuous life (1323a38–b21).

This leaves open the question of which virtues he has in mind, so in chapter 2 he summarises the two options: those of the political and the contemplative lives (1324a25–35), though he then proceeds to devote the rest of the chapter to considering and rejecting an extreme (or perverted) form of the political life, one that involves mastery over neighbouring states and nations. Such is the life pursued by those who make war their principal aim, like the Spartans (1324b2–1325a7). But in chapter 3 he returns to the two options outlined at 1324a25–35 and considers the objections that advocates of one make against the other.

Those who reject the political life think that the exercise of power is inconsistent with the life of a freeman. Presumably, the objection is that it is too demanding. Aristotle has two responses. The first is continuous with the theme of the previous chapter. Political rule is not despotic and does not involve treating fellow citizens as slaves (1325a24–31): if it did, that would constitute a problem for the political life, because there is nothing noble in managing slaves, and giving orders to them is merely necessary. But this is not what defines the political life.[55] Second, one should not aim for political rule without limit (which would be too demanding) but hold offices only for limited periods, stepping back to allow other citizens to take their turn, as long as they are equal in virtue (1325a34–b14).

Where contemplation is concerned, Aristotle is keen to rebut the misconception (espoused both by some of its proponents and opponents) that it is inactive. Thinking, he argues, is a kind of activity, especially thinking that has no goal beyond itself. He agrees that *eudaimonia* must consist in activity and, so long as contemplation is correctly described as activity, it remains a candidate for the good life (1325b16–23).

In these two chapters, *Pol.* VII 2–3, Aristotle does not rule out one option in favour of the other; both politics and contemplation remain in the field. What he does is to refute bad arguments against each of them, as well as to exclude the extreme and distorted view of the political life, the life of imperial domination.

---

[55] See Kraut (1997) 70 for a good description of the line of argument here.

The next several chapters (4–12) take up more practical topics concerned with the ideal state (e.g. population, territory and property), but chapters 13–15 return to more general questions about the definition of *eudaimonia*. In this section, he also returns to the comparison between moral-cum-political activity and contemplation. His focus here is partly on virtue: what kinds of virtue should the statesman aim to inculcate in his citizens and how will he do so? Central to his discussion of virtue and happiness is the concept of leisure (*scholē*). States and individuals reach their highest goal when they are in a state of leisure, not when they are at war or working to secure life's necessities. This affects our assessment of the different virtues. Courage is necessary in war, but not in peace; it is not leisurely. By contrast, the virtue of *philosophia* comes into play only when we are at peace, with an adequate supply of external goods. (Temperance and justice stand between these extremes, playing a role in times of both war and peace.) Since *philosophia* is purely leisurely, unlike courage, temperance and justice, we may be tempted to infer that, as in *NE* X 7–8, Aristotle ranks contemplation over moral-cum-political activity. However, scholars are divided as to whether he says as much explicitly. I shall return to this point shortly.

As well as looking at *Pol.* VII, we shall also be drawing on other parts of the work when we come to discuss the question of whether civic *eudaimonia* is aggregative or organic in nature. A few of these come from book VII, which sometimes touches on the relation between individual and civic happiness, but there are also passages in books I–III that contain important material about the nature and goals of the state.

Since we shall be reading passages from the *NE* and the *Politics* side by side, the question arises of the relation between the two works. It is sometimes thought that they are continuous, the *Politics* being written as the sequel to the *NE*: first, Aristotle gives an account of the good life; then he works out how this might be realised in the state.[56] However, the *Politics* cannot be treated so straightforwardly as the second volume of a project started in the *NE*. True, the *NE* closes with a promise to look at certain political topics (X 9, 1181a15–23), and this does sound rather like a table of contents for the *Politics*, though the match is not perfect.[57] Furthermore, there are important discrepancies between the two works, especially when it comes to *Pol.* VII, which contains views at odds with the *NE* concerning such topics as philosophical method, moral psychology and education.[58] At the

---

[56] Rowe (1991) 72 and Salkever (2009a) 209.

[57] The list of topics in *NE* X 9 fails to mention the discussion of the household in *Pol.* I.

[58] I have discussed these in Scott (2015) 177–86 as well as in (2020) 127–29 and 160–63. Like Kraut (1997) 129 and (2002) 16–19, I believe parts of the *Politics* could have been written before parts of the *NE*, which would help to explain these discrepancies.

same time, there are substantial areas of overlap. But it is safest not to start out with the blanket assumption that the two works are written to complement one another. There is one topic on which we need to decide at the outset whether the two texts agree. This is the question of whether in the *Politics* Aristotle considers contemplation superior to moral activity, as he does in *NE* X 7–8. As I have just said, scholars are divided on this point, but here I wish to argue in favour of convergence. The problem is that, when he discusses contemplation and compares it with political activity in *Pol.* VII 2–3 and 14–15, he seems to avoid committing himself on the issue. In fact, however, a careful reading of a passage in VII 3 shows him putting contemplation in first place:

> If we are right in our view, and happiness is assumed to be virtuous activity, the active life will be the best, both for every city collectively, and for individuals. Not that a life of action must necessarily have relation to others, as some persons think, nor are those ideas only to be regarded as practical which are pursued for the sake of practical results, *but much more the thoughts and contemplations which are independent and complete in themselves.* (1325b14–21, emphasis added)

Although Aristotle makes no reference to the divinity of contemplation, he does point to the fact that it constitutes *praxis* in its fullest sense: it is 'complete in itself' because it aims at no further end. Since *eudaimonia* consists in virtuous *praxis*, this constitutes an argument for ranking contemplation over political activity. So, in what follows, I shall assume that the *Politics* and the *NE* agree on which life is superior, even though the latter is much more forthright on the issue.[59]

3.1.2 The Value of Contemplation for the Individual

As in Section 2, it will help our discussion of the civic value of contemplation if we start with its value for the individual. Obviously, there is a huge amount that could be said here, but my interest is narrower in focus: what kind of value does it have – intrinsic, instrumental, or both? The answer seems clear, both from *NE* X 7 and *Pol.* VII 14–15: contemplation has only intrinsic value.

As we have just seen, *NE* X 7 is mostly taken up with a series of arguments for the superiority of contemplation over the practical life. There are two of them that are relevant here. One states the very point I wish to make, that contemplation is chosen only for its own sake, not for any further consequence (1177b1–4). This recalls one of the formal criteria for *eudaimonia* stated in I 7 (1097a28–b6):

---

[59] Here I agree with Roochnik (2008) 724 and 726–28, esp. 726: 'the theoretical life is the highest form of *praxis*.' See also Barker (1946) 320. By contrast, Kraut (1997) appears ambivalent on the issue. On p. 139 he concedes that 1325b16–21 hints at the superiority of contemplation, but on p. 74 he says that Aristotle does not emphasise the point or use it to argue for the superiority of contemplation.

eudaimonia, the human good, must be an end (*telos*) in the fullest sense. Aristotle states that some things are choiceworthy only for a further end, others only for their own sake, and others are choiceworthy in both ways (1097b30–34). But whatever counts as most 'end-like' goal (*teleiotaton*) is something that is purely an end, never a means. And this must be true of *eudaimonia*. So, when in X 7 he comes to state his considered position on which activity most satisfies the conditions for being *eudaimonia*, he selects contemplation because (among other things) it fits this criterion perfectly. At the same time, he contrasts moral or political activities as having goals outside of themselves. They are not as 'end-like': courage, for example, has the further goal of securing peace.[60]

A closely associated argument for the supremacy of contemplation concerns the concept of leisure (X 7, 1177b4–15). Aristotle associates *eudaimonia* with leisure rather than work. He then claims that, while contemplation is something we pursue when we are at leisure, the moral and political virtues are non-leisurely (1177b7–8): we engage in them in so far as there is some need to address. Again, courage is a good example.

Both these arguments underline the point that, for an individual, contemplation has no instrumental value. And they can each be found in *Pol* VII. We have already seen the first argument at work in VII 3, 1325b16–21, and the argument about leisure appears in *Pol.* VII 14–15. Here, he distinguishes virtues in terms of leisure or its absence.[61] When one is at leisure, one does not attempt to fulfil any particular need; the activities pursued in leisure must be choiceworthy for their own sakes. If contemplation is only leisurely (unlike activities involving courage and temperance), it must be choiceworthy for its own sake alone: if it had some further benefit (as it does in Plato's *Republic*), it would straddle the divide between leisure and work. To this extent, *Pol.* VII 14–15, like VII 3, echo the arguments in *NE* X 7, 1177b1–4 and 1177b4–15 that contemplation, unlike the activities of the moral virtues, is pursued for itself alone and associated entirely with leisure.

Part of the explanation for his claiming that contemplation has no instrumental value lies in the way he differentiates theoretical knowledge from practical reason. At *NE* VI 12, 1143b19–20, he states that wisdom (*sophia*) does not study the sources of human *eudaimonia*, because it is not concerned with how

---

[60] Oddly, in *NE* X 7, 1177b17–18, he says that none of the moral virtues is pursued for its own sake, only for the sake of something beyond itself (cf. also 1177b1–2). This conflicts with earlier claims in the work that morally virtuous action is choiceworthy for its own sake (as well as its consequences). See Bostock (2000) 193–95 for further discussion of the problem. It is as if Aristotle overstates the case against moral virtue here in X 7. For our purposes, we can leave the puzzle to one side: our focus is on the kind of value that Aristotle's attributes to contemplation.

[61] 1334a19–36. Or to be more precise, he operates with a set of three distinctions: war and peace, work and leisure, the necessary and the noble. See Kraut (1997) 141.

things come into being. Conversely, throughout *NE* VI, he insists that the virtue of practical reason, *phronēsis*, is not a matter of applying theoretical knowledge (*nous*, *epistēmē* or *sophia*). It is a different form of knowledge, which he sometimes characterises as a kind of perception (cf. VI 8, 1142a27–30), even if it also involves universal judgements to shape practical judgements. This contrasts starkly with the approach of the *Republic*, as we saw in Sections 2.2 and 2.3: for Plato, good practical reasoning is essentially the application of theoretical knowledge, while Aristotle thinks of it as a distinct and autonomous state or capacity, which could be possessed and exercised even if one had no theoretical wisdom at all.[62]

By separating theoretical from practical reasoning in this way, Aristotle makes contemplation – both contemplative knowledge and the activity itself – useless for practical decision making.[63] As a result, the only value that contemplation can have for the individual is intrinsic. We saw in Section 2.4 (n. 13) that it can have intrinsic value while also contributing to *eudaimonia*. But this is because it is a component of *eudaimonia*; it does not help produce it in an instrumental sense.

What about other ways of applying theoretical knowledge than trying to use it to support moral reasoning – that is, technological uses of scientific knowledge? In the *NE* Aristotle does not mention the idea of using contemplative knowledge in this way, though in *Pol.* I 11, 1259a5–21 he does cite the example of Thales

---

[62] See *Pol.* VII 14, 1333a27–9, where he implies that some people are incapable of contemplation, but capable of moral activity based on the possession of *phronēsis*.

[63] See Nagel (1980) 12, Wilkes (1980) 347–48, Broadie (1991) 392, and Nightingale (2004) 198 and 203. In a wide-ranging study, Walker (2018) pits himself against this consensus: see esp. ch. 7, where he argues that 'contemplative *nous* authoritatively guides practical reason' (p. 129). But there are good reasons for siding with the orthodoxy on this occasion. At various points in the *NE*, Aristotle places limits on the extent to which practical reasoning should aspire to the methods of theoretical science: see I 6, 1096b26–31; I 7, 1098a26–b3; I 13, 1102a23–32; X 4, 1174b2–4; and X 8, 1178a20–3. He does so under two headings: practical reasoning should not expect the same degree of precision (*akribeia*) as theoretical science and should not pursue the quest for explanation to the same extent. (I have discussed these two kinds of restriction in Scott (2015) ch. 7 and ch. 8 respectively.) Walker interprets Aristotle to mean not that practical reasoning in general should eschew the same level of precision as theoretical wisdom, but that he 'brackets more detailed psychological inquiry in the *Nicomachean Ethics* momentarily, for pedagogical reasons' (p. 135). But this conflicts with what Aristotle says in I 7, 1098a26–33: 'And we must also remember what has been said before, and not look for precision in all things alike, but in each class of things such precision as accords with the subject matter, and so much as is appropriate to the inquiry.' Here the reason for limiting the degree of precision is not pedagogical but arises from the underlying subject matter. In the same place he adds: 'Nor must we demand the explanation in all matters alike; it is enough that in some cases the fact be well established' (1098a33–b2). Again, this limits the extent to which practical reasoning should reach back towards first principles: it no more needs to go back to fundamental explanations than a carpenter needs to study geometry, to use the parallel that Aristotle invoked in the preceding lines. Since this restriction on explanation follows immediately after the one on precision, it would be very implausible to say that it is only temporary, imposed for pedagogical purposes, rather than a point about the underlying subject-matter, as before. For similar reservations about Walker's approach, see Harbin (2019) 407, Rabinoff (2019) 488, Curzer (2020) 214–45 and Hirji (2020) 468.

using astronomy to predict a bumper olive harvest. Then, by renting all the olive presses at a low cost before the harvest, he created a monopoly for himself and made a great deal of money when it came. So, we might suppose, Aristotle ought to soften his anti-instrumentalism about theoretical knowledge and modify it to accommodate such examples. I shall postpone further discussion of this issue until the end of Section 4, once we have looked more closely at what counts as contemplation (Section 4.5).[64]

3.2 Aristotle on Civic *Eudaimonia*

We are now ready to address our central question: even if contemplating is intrinsically good for the individual, how is it good for the state? (For all the reasons just given, it cannot have instrumental value for the state, any more than it does for the individual.) But how exactly does it contribute intrinsic value in this context? I shall pose the question in terms of civic *eudaimonia*. In *Pol.* VII 1–2, Aristotle assumes that happiness or *eudaimonia* is a property that applies to the state and that a state reaches its *telos* when it attains happiness. So how does contemplation contribute to the *eudaimonia* of the state?

To answer this question, I wish to follow a similar strategy as before when dealing with the *Republic*. I shall start with the question of whether civic *eudaimonia* is merely an aggregate reducible to the happiness of the individuals within it, or whether it is organic in character. If we take the aggregative view, it becomes easy to see why individual contemplation is good for the state. Merely by contemplating, citizens can in principle add to the sum of happiness. If we take the organic view, matters will be less straightforward: we need to determine what the organic property of civic *eudaimonia* consists in and then establish how contemplation contributes to it.

The question of which view of civic *eudaimonia* Aristotle took is at least as vexed as with the *Republic*. Our texts seem to point us in both directions, and there is currently little consensus on the issue. By way of an introduction, I shall

---

[64] Famous though it is, one can question how well Thales' story illustrates the practical application of theoretical science. First, his use of astronomy applies only to his prediction about the harvest; the main point of the anecdote concerns his insight into monopolistic pricing, which is not said to derive from any theoretical science. Second, is the astronomy that he used a theoretical science? In *An. Po.* I 13, 78b39–79a1, Aristotle distinguishes between astronomy proper and merely recording the movements of the stars (observational astronomy). In the same place, he also distinguishes between mathematical and nautical astronomy. (The latter is perhaps very close to observational astronomy, as Ross (1949) 555 suggests.) It was presumably this empirical approach that Thales was using, not the mathematical and highly abstract kind praised as being close to first philosophy at *Met.* XII 8, 1073b5–8. (In the ancient world people regularly tried to correlate astronomical data with weather patterns: on 'astrometereology', see Taub (2003) 16–20.) Nonetheless, even if Thales is not such a good example, Aristotle must still have been interested in the possibility of theoretical sciences yielding technological results.

give a sample of texts that have been used to support the aggregative view and then turn to passages that seem to point towards the organic one.

3.2.1 Evidence for the Aggregative View

Scholars have claimed to find evidence for the aggregative interpretation in the *Politics*, especially books II and VII.[65] The first of these is devoted to examining previous political theories, among them the account of the ideal state in the *Republic* (*Pol.* II 2–5). In chapter 2, he criticises Socrates for aiming to make the city as unified as possible. (For Aristotle, a city-state is essentially a plurality, whereas Socrates' obsession with maximizing unity threatens to turn it into something other than a city – a household or even an individual: cf. 1261a15–22.) In chapters 3–5, he objects to the means by which Socrates proposes to achieve this unity: the communism of women and children (chapters 3–4) and the communism of property (chapter 5). Leaving aside whether Aristotle's interpretation of the *Republic* is accurate, we can use it to expose his own assumptions about the relation between individual and civic happiness. A particularly revealing passage comes towards the end of II 5:

> Again, he deprives the guardians even of happiness, and says that the legislator ought to make the whole state happy. But the whole cannot be happy unless most, or all, or some of its parts enjoy happiness. In this respect happiness is not like the even principle in numbers, which may exist only in the whole, but in neither of the parts; not so happiness. And if the guardians are not happy, who are? Surely not the artisans, or the common people. (1264b15–24)

This shows that for Aristotle a city cannot be happy unless at least some parts of it are, and that he perceived this as a key point of difference with the *Republic*. In some way, and to some extent, civic happiness tracks individual happiness.

Some commentators have used this passage to show that Aristotle held an aggregative account of civic *eudaimonia*. If the happiness of the state requires the happiness of some, if not all, of its citizens, perhaps this is because he thought happiness is purely a function of the happiness of the individual citizens – the sum of their happiness.[66]

Scholars have given further support to this view by considering what civic happiness consists in. As we have seen, Aristotle argues that civic happiness takes the same form as individual happiness (*Pol.* VII 2, 1324a5–13; cf. also *NE* I 2, 1094b7–8). Since the latter consists in activity in accordance with virtue, the same should hold for civic happiness. Now consider the following claim about civic virtue:

---

[65] See Miller (1995) esp. 198–204 and Kraut (2002) 213–14.
[66] See Kraut (2002) 213; perhaps also Miller (1995) 210.

> A city is good through the citizens who have a share in the government being good. (VII 13, 1332a32–4)

Here, civic virtue arises 'through' the virtue of individuals. This could mean that a virtuous state is analysable into a state of virtuous citizens. Civic happiness would then follow suit: when enough individual citizens act in accordance with their virtue (and so attain happiness), the city is thereby acting likewise and hence happy. Again, this leads us straight to the aggregative view of civic *eudaimonia*.[67]

These two passages talk directly about a civic property (viz. happiness or goodness) and link it to the existence of the corresponding property in individual citizens. Advocates of the aggregative interpretation have also cited a couple of texts from early on in *Pol.* VII that make a connection between the constitution of the ideal state and individual happiness:

> He who would duly inquire about the best constitution ought first to determine which is the most choiceworthy life; while this remains uncertain the best form of the state must also be uncertain; for, in the natural order of things, those may be expected to lead the best life who are governed in the best manner of which their circumstances admit. (VII 1, 1323a14–19)

> It is evident that the best constitution is that in which every person, whoever he is, can act best and live happily. (VII 2, 1324a23–5)[68]

The first text seems to assume that the purpose of the best state is to promote the best life for individual citizens; that is why an investigation into best constitution needs to be premised on an understanding of the best life for an individual. The second text likewise makes it sound as if the purpose of the constitution is to make the citizens individually happy. If we then ask why the legislator aims at the happiness of each and every one of the citizens, the aggregative view is ready with an answer: civic happiness, which constitutes the legislator's ultimate goal, just is the aggregate of individual happiness.

3.2.2 A Signal in Favour of the Organic View: Pol. I 2

Scholars are by no means unanimous about adopting the aggregative interpretation, and certainly none of the above texts shows Aristotle explicitly committing himself to this view. So instead, some advocate an organic approach: civic happiness is a fact about the way the city is structured, not a mere amalgam of the happiness of its individual citizens.

---

[67] Miller (1995) discusses this passage at 222–23.
[68] Miller (1995) 214 uses the second text to support the aggregative interpretation. Nussbaum (1988) 147–8 interprets both texts this way, even though she finds evidence for an organic interpretation of civic happiness elsewhere in the *Politics*. See below n. 91.

Consider this very famous passage from the second chapter of the *Politics*:

> Further, the state is by nature clearly prior to the family and to the individual, since the whole is of necessity prior to the part; for example, if the whole body be destroyed, there will be no foot or hand, except in an equivocal sense, as we might speak of a stone hand; for when destroyed the hand will be no better than that. But things are defined by their working and power; and we ought not to say that they are the same when they no longer have their proper quality, but only that they have the same name. The proof that the state is a creation of nature and prior to the individual is that the individual, when isolated, is not self-sufficing; and therefore he is like a part in relation to the whole. But he who is unable to live in society, or who has no need because he is sufficient for himself, must be either a beast or a god: he is no part of a state. (*Pol.* I 2, 1253a18–29)

When introducing the organic theory of the state in Section 2.5.1, I said that it has two components: one concerns whether the state itself is an organic entity, the other whether its happiness is an organic property. The *Republic* contains no explicit discussion of the ontology of the state, though there are comments bearing on the property of civic happiness. In Aristotle's case, things are different. This passage, at least, has been taken as a bold statement about the ontology of the state to the effect that the *polis* is a natural, organic entity, on a par with a living body – a hylomorphic entity akin to other natural organisms, the matter being the inhabitants; the form the constitution.[69] Other scholars think that there is too much a gap between the *polis* and Aristotle's views on natural organisms elsewhere and argue that the analogy between the state and a body should be taken only loosely.[70]

As before, I do not wish to enter into the debate about the ontology of the state. But I do wish to use this passage to make a point about what kind of property civic happiness should be taken to be. It is not pressing the analogy too far to say that Aristotle sees the state as having a *telos* that is achieved when its individual citizens, its parts, are behaving in the appropriate ways. This strongly suggests that the civic *telos*, presumably civic *eudaimonia*, involves structured, inter-related activity on the part of its citizens. After all, a body is a teleologically organised system, not a mere collection of health-ily functioning parts;[71] similarly, the happiness of the state, its *telos*, does not reduce to the fact of all the citizens individually performing actions in accordance with virtue, which would be what an aggregate of individual

---

[69] Reeve (1998) lv–lvi, Morrison (2013) 188 and Segev (2017) 100. For an extended discussion of the state as a natural entity in Aristotle, see Keyt (1987).
[70] E.g. Mayhew (1997), Kullman (1991) and Pellegrin (2015) 45.
[71] See Newman (1902) III 131–32 and Barker (1946) 96 commenting on *Pol.* III 1, 1274b38–40.

happiness would amount to.[72] On this basis, it seems appropriate to ask whether there is other evidence in the *Politics* for seeing civic *eudaimonia* as an organic property.[73]

3.2.3 The Organic View of Secondary Eudaimonia

To develop this suggestion, there are different ways we could go. One would be metaphysical: try to pin down precisely what sort of entity Aristotle conceives the state to be; then explore the nature of the properties it can possess, such as *eudaimonia*. A less ambitious route to follow would be ethical: whatever he thinks about the ontology of the state, how does he define civic *eudaimonia*?[74] I shall follow this second, shorter, route. Our starting point should be that happiness is the same for state and individual. So we can immediately turn to his views about individual *eudaimonia* as a guide. (He has far more to say about the former than the latter.) Given that individual happiness is activity in accordance with virtue, civic happiness must involve civic action based on civic virtue (cf. VII 3, 1325b14–16). No surprise then that Aristotle says, 'the happy city may be shown to be that which is best and which acts rightly' (VII 1, 1323b30–31).

Now we need to introduce another fundamental point. As we have seen, in *NE* X 7–8 he splits individual *eudaimonia* into two kinds, primary and secondary – contemplative and practical (i.e. moral-cum-political). Presumably, therefore, civic *eudaimonia* will also have two kinds. And these two kinds are based on different sets of virtues: the virtues of the theoretical intellect for primary *eudaimonia* and, for the secondary kind, *phronēsis* and the virtues of character.

The next step is to investigate the nature of civic virtue. For the moment, I shall leave aside primary *eudaimonia* and the virtues of theoretical reason in order to focus on the practical virtues. Almost immediately after the text I just quoted, Aristotle says:

> Thus the courage, justice, and wisdom of a state have the same form and nature as the qualities which give the individual who possesses them the name of just, wise, or temperate. (VII 1, 1323b33–6)

---

[72] Some scholars who take the aggregative approach allow for a certain degree of structure to emerge once the individual citizens act virtuously; many of the virtues are distinctly social in character. See e.g. Miller (1995) 200–204 for a discussion of these strategies. But the analogy used in *Pol.* I 2 suggests something stronger: not that the structure emerges from the bottom up, but that Aristotle takes a top-down approach.

[73] I shall also discuss the civic *telos* in the appendix to this part (Section 3.3).

[74] In Section 3.2.1, we cited some texts bearing on the question of how civic happiness is related to individual happiness, but this is not the same as the more basic question of its definition.

According to Martha Nussbaum, this expresses the principle that a 'political arrangement is good (or virtuous in some concrete respect) just in case it has the same structure that is the structure of goodness (or some concrete virtue) in the soul of an individual human being.'[75] I agree with this view and accept that it implies an organic conception of civic virtue, rather than the aggregative one. Another scholar who takes this line is Donald Morrison:

> The courage, justice, and other virtues of the individual have counterparts in the courage, justice, and other virtues of the city itself. But the city's virtue does not consist in some number of the citizens that has virtue.[76]

If virtue is to be understood in this organic way, activity in accordance with virtue (i.e. *eudaimonia*) should follow suit. When a city acts, especially the ideal state, the action is the result of a structured decision-making process: the leaders follow due process and their subordinates, duly appointed, follow up on their decisions. This is not a mere aggregate of virtuous actions.[77]

All this is by way of an outline. We can develop it further if we acknowledge that Aristotle had his own version of the state-soul parallel so pronounced in the *Republic*.[78] When discussing the sorts of relationships that should hold between different groups of people, he sometimes invokes parallels with the relation between parts of individuals. He compares the intrapersonal relation that holds between reason and the affective part[79] of the soul with the sort of relationship that holds between rulers and subjects in the state.[80] This is most explicit in *Pol.* I 5:

> At all events we may firstly observe in living creatures both a despotical and a constitutional rule; for the soul rules the body with a despotical rule, whereas the intellect rules the appetites with a constitutional and royal rule. And it is clear that the rule of the soul over the body, and of the mind and the

---

[75] Nussbaum (1988) 155–56. On p. 158, she writes: this principle 'allows that a city is good just in case its parts have a certain relation to one another that makes an overall structure that is similar to the structure of goodness in an individual soul.'

[76] Morrison (2017) 16.

[77] As Morrison (2017) 17–18 argues. See also Segev (2017) 100–102. Lockwood (2019) 19–23 disputes whether a state's action should be understood organically but does believe that the life (*bios*) of the state is to be understood in organic terms.

[78] As I argued in Scott (2015) 13–15, it is better to use the term 'parallel' than 'analogy' when describing Plato's views on the relation between state and soul. In the *Republic*, justice in the state is the same form as justice in the soul (IV 435a6–9), not an analogue of it. The same applies to the other virtues. As we have just seen from *Pol.* VII 1, 1323b33–6, Aristotle agrees with him regarding the identity of the virtues in state and soul.

[79] The *alogon*, the seat of appetite and the emotions (*NE* I 13, 1102b29–31).

[80] On Aristotle's state-soul parallel, see Spelman (1983) 21; Reeve (1998) lxi; Garsten (2013) 211–12, 214, and 216; and Frank (2015) 12 and 24. Aristotle is more cautious about pressing the comparison than Plato, not least because he thinks the kind of unity involved in state and soul is different (*Pol.* II 2, 1261a15–22).

rational element over the passionate, is natural and expedient; whereas the equality of the two or the rule of the inferior is always hurtful.[81]

An individual is happy when they possess the virtues of both parts of the soul, rational and affective, and act in accordance with these virtues. The happy person has *phronēsis*, which they use in controlling their appetites, emotions and actions. Being morally virtuous, they are not encratic: they do not have recalcitrant feelings that have to be supressed. By analogy, the citizen body of the state has ruling and subject parts. The city will be virtuous when its subject part falls into line with its ruling part. In essence, this is what its virtue consists in. Similarly, when its actions express this structural feature, or 'fall out' of this state of harmony, it achieves happiness – activity arising from a structural harmony between groups of citizens. Unlike on the aggregative account, neither its virtue nor its happiness consists in, or reduces to, the virtue or happiness of individual citizens.

Now, we saw (Section 3.2.1) that a happy city requires the existence of happy citizens – if not all, then at least some (II 5, 1264b15–24). Similarly, the city's virtue, on which its happiness depends, requires the existence of virtue among individual citizens (VII 13, 1332a32–4). How does the conception of civic happiness that I am developing explain this?

The answer is that, for the state to enjoy the sort of harmony just outlined, most citizens, whether rulers or subjects, must themselves possess the virtues individually and act in accordance with them. The rulers must possess *phronēsis*, especially 'architectonic' reason (cf. *Pol.* I 13, 1260a18–19); the subjects possess the moral virtues, but these are 'servant' virtues: they involve submitting to the prescriptions of their rulers, performing the requisite actions and being affected in the appropriate way.[82] As we have seen, the subjects are willing subjects; they do not resent or in any way attempt to undermine their rulers; otherwise, the city would not be virtuous (and happy), but encratic.

Also, Aristotle thinks that the rulers should be in their middle age and that the young should be ruled (*Pol.* VII 9, 1329a2–17 and 14, 1332b34–41). But when the young grow older, they in turn will hold office, though they do not entirely leave behind the possibility of being subjects again: since the ideal state involves freemen ruling over freemen (*Pol.* VII 14, 1332b25–7), even those who exercise their *phronēsis* in office must regularly cede their power so that others can rule. What this means is that the citizens of the best state (at different

---

[81] For some other passages that suggest a parallel between state and soul (or between the interpersonal and the intra-personal), see *NE* VI 7, 1140a25–8, VI 13, 1145a9–11 and IX 8, 1168b28–34; *Pol.* I 12 and I 13, 1260a4–8; cf. also VII 3, 1325b27–8.

[82] Of course, the comparison needs to be a little more complicated than this: the rulers do not just possess *phronēsis*, but also have the moral virtues; and the subjects do not lack rationality but have true opinion. See *Pol.* III 4, 1277b28–9.

stages in their lives) will typically possess and act in accordance with either the servant virtues or genuine virtue (backed by *phronēsis*).[83] They will possess happiness of some kind or other – to the degree of which they are capable.

Here we have an account of the good of the state which could be called 'organic': civic happiness is not analysed as an aggregate property; it does not consist in the fact of most citizens being happy. At the same time, it requires that they are (mostly) happy. Individual and civic happiness march in step.[84]

Not only does civic happiness require that most citizens are individually happy; it seems plausible to say that the more citizens that are happy, the happier the state will be. If, at the extreme, all the citizens possess virtue and act in accordance with it, the state's happiness will be completely unimpeded. By contrast, if there were some 'rotten apples' among the citizenry, there would be more obstacles to virtuous activity.

3.2.4 Contemplation and Organic Eudaimonia

In discussing what it means for a state to enjoy civic *eudaimonia*, I have so far focused solely on its possession of *phronēsis* and the moral virtues. But how are we to incorporate theoretical contemplation into the picture? What is it for a state to possess the virtues of theoretical reason and actualise them?

To answer this, we need to show how contemplation is integrated into the life of the state. There might seem to be a problem here. In *NE* X, Aristotle seems to present it as a rather solitary activity, less bound up with our nature as social beings – our anthropic nature – and more connected to our divine element (Aristotle's god is not a social being). True, we do need other people to help us engage in the activity, but the way he phrases the point in *NE* X 7, 1177a32–b1 makes it sound like a concession: here he remarks that contemplation is the most 'self-sufficient' of activities, in the sense that it depends less on other people than moral and political activity; and that this is a mark in favour of its candidacy to be perfect *eudaimonia*. But if contemplation is at its core asocial, how can it truly be integrated into the life of the state?

It could be said that Aristotle even encourages us to raise this problem. In *Pol.* I 2, he claims that human beings are political animals (1253a1–18 and 27–9). This is bound up with his analogy between the state and a body (1253a18–27),

---

[83] There is the question of how servant virtues relate to citizen-virtue, which is distinguished from full moral virtue in *Pol.* III 4, 1277b7–30; cf. also I 13, 1260a14–24. I do not have space to pursue that question here, but for a helpful discussion, see Rosler (2013) 147–49.

[84] This shows how it is possible to espouse an organic theory of civic *eudaimonia*, while holding extra assumptions that entail the impossibility of the whole being happy unless all (or most of) the parts are. Aristotle's complaint against Plato in *Pol.* II 5, 1264b15–24 is not that he takes an organic approach to civic happiness, but that he wrongly makes unity the *summum bonum*.

which implies that citizens are parts of a whole contributing to its health (i.e. its *eudaimonia*). As political animals, we have a natural urge to live in a community (1253a29–30): we seek to be part of something bigger than ourselves and co-operate to secure a communal goal. When he talks of humans as political animals here, it is quite natural to take him to be referring to what he calls our 'composite nature' in *NE* X 8, 1178a9–22, which involves the anthropic qualities of practical reason and the moral virtues. (It is through exercising the anthropic virtues as individuals that we bring about the secondary happiness of the ideal state.) To clarify what is meant by a 'political animal', *Pol.* I 2 also draws a contrast with someone who lives as a stateless individual: politically speaking, an alien, who is compared to an isolated piece in a game of draughts (1253a4–5). At the end of this passage, Aristotle says that such a person would be either a beast or a god (1253a 27–9). Presumably, they are a beast if it is appetite that renders them unfit for society (cf. *NE* VII 5 on 'bestiality' as a character state, ranked even lower than moral vice). But why would he also compare them to a god? An obvious answer is that they pursue the contemplative life, presented as divine and solitary in *NE* X 7–8. But if this is what he has in mind, has he not admitted that the person who enjoys perfect *eudaimonia* is in effect no longer a political animal and no longer part of the state?

But it cannot be right to see contemplation as an activity divorced from the political sphere. This is immediately clear from the fact that in *Pol.* VII Aristotle is very interested in the role of contemplation as part of his discussion of the ideal state: promoting the virtue of philosophy and with it the activity of contemplation is integral to realising civic happiness. The same applies to the *NE*, although the point has sometimes been overlooked. Despite the appearance of the word 'ethics' in its title (which, as far as we know was not Aristotle's), the treatise is consistently framed as a work of political science (*politikē*), written to help promote happiness in the state.[85] This is made clear very early in the work. The first chapter sets out the overall topic of the treatise: the human good, the final goal of all our choices and activities; the second identifies the discipline to which the treatise belongs. The answer is that it is a work of politics, and its beneficiary will be someone trying to promote the good of the state, not primarily of the individual (I 2, 1094b7–11). And this is not a one-off comment. When he refers to the general character of the work, Aristotle describes it as political or legislative;[86] he never uses the term 'ethical' to describe his overall

---

[85]   On this, see Scott (2015) 106–15, with references on p. 107 n. 4 to Burnet (1900) xxvii, Hardie (1980) 28, Bodéüs (1993) ch. 1, Kraut (2002) 3–19, Schofield (2006a) and Frede (2013).

[86]   As well as I 2, 1094b11, see I 3, 1095a2–3, I 13, 1102a5–9, and VII 11, 1152b1–3); also I 9, 1099b28–32, II 3, 1105a10–13, and III 1, 1109b34–5.

project. Because the discussion of contemplation in books VI and X is integral to the analysis of the overall goal at which the statesman is to aim, it is his role to spread possibilities for contemplation within the state.[87] So there is no way that Aristotle can think of the contemplative life as essentially contrasted with the civic life. When the statesman fosters contemplation among his citizens, he is not turning them into political aliens.

So how should contemplation be woven into the life of the state? Contrast two types of state. In one, a number of inhabitants engage in contemplation, but they do so quite independently of the state (cf. *Rep.* VII 520b3). Perhaps the authorities are unaware of their activity; certainly, they have no interest in it and do nothing to support it. But Aristotle's ideal state will not be like this. As we have just seen, contemplation will be considered a goal for statesmen to promote. It may not be the only goal, but it is still of great importance, perhaps the highest goal, towards which the city as a whole is working.[88] This is quite different from the city where intellectual activity might happen to occur, despite the indifference (or even hostility) of the rulers.

There is another way in which contemplation is integrated into the life of the ideal city. Here we turn directly to the people engaging in contemplation. Although it is easy to think of the contemplator as an alien, an outsider (not unlike the travelling sophists, roaming from one state to another), the people who engage in contemplation in Aristotle's ideal state are very much citizens.[89] There is a distinction between leading the contemplative life, in the sense of doing only that, and engaging in contemplation alongside other more social activities. This is what Aristotle recommends we do in *NE* X 8, 1178b5–6: 'in so far as he is a human being and lives with a number of people, he chooses to do virtuous acts.' For contemplation to be an integral part of the ideal state, those who engage in it must themselves be integrated into the city. There is no reason why this cannot be the case.

The upshot of this is that the 'divine alien' referred to at the end of *Pol.* I 2 is quite different from the kind of citizen whom the statesman will encourage to contemplate in the ideal state; and we should resist the temptation to assimilate the contrast between the political animal and the divine alien drawn in *Pol.* I 2 to

---

[87] On the instrumental value of *phronēsis* in promoting contemplation, see *NE* VI 13, 1145a6–9: *phronēsis* 'is not supreme over philosophic wisdom (*sophia*), i.e. over the superior part of us, any more than the art of medicine is over health; for it does not use it but provides for its coming into being; it issues orders, then, for its sake, but not to it'. Although Aristotle's immediate focus here is on the individual, his remarks will apply to the way the leaders use their political *phronēsis* to facilitate contemplation within the state (cf. VI 8, 1141b23–1142a10). The political implications of *NE* VI 13, 1145a6–11 are brought out by Broadie and Rowe (2002) 384.

[88] Cooper (2010) 263 argues that even citizens who do not engage in contemplation themselves come to share in the good that it represents by supporting it with their morally virtuous activity.

[89] Reeve (1998) xlvii. Contrast Roochnik (2008) 731–35.

the distinction between the two lives made in *NE* X 7–8. True, the political animal described in *Pol.* I 2 does represent the 'composite' soul of *NE* X 8, who possesses the anthropic virtues. But the stateless alien likened to a god in *Pol.* I 2, 1253a29 is not meant to be identified with the person who exercises the contemplative virtues in in *NE* X 7–8. The 'divine alien' of *Pol.* I 2 is more like the first kind of contemplator we described earlier: a stateless intellectual.[90] The second kind of contemplator, fully engaged in the life of the city, is not under consideration in *Pol.* I 2.

So, in the ideal state, contemplation is something around which the city is structured: it is consciously promoted and sustained by the political leaders, as well as supported and endorsed by the citizens quite generally; and those who engage in it are fully fledged citizens, the same people who serve on assemblies and help promote contemplative activity. As long as these conditions hold, we can say that a state like this is a contemplative state and enjoys supreme *eudaimonia*.

Even so, it is not clear how well contemplation fits into the organic view of civic happiness, rather than the aggregative one. I have established two conditions that need to be met for a state to be considered contemplative. But once they are met, what is actually going on when the state 'contemplates'? Surely it is no more than that a group of citizens individually contemplate, albeit with state sponsorship and support. There is a clear contrast between this activity and moral-cum-political activity. There, the activity essentially involves interrelations between groups of citizens, making the case for an organic view of civic happiness strong. But theoretical activity is simpler: it does not involve one element interacting with another. So the aggregative view is more suited to this kind of activity than the organic.

This may seem a very surprising result: Aristotle, it turns out, favours both the organic and aggregative accounts of civic happiness. But this is not at all implausible. The root of the matter is that he posits two types of *eudaimonia*, primary and secondary. In *NE* X 8, he argues that an individual should aspire to include both types in their life. When we turn to civic happiness, which he thinks takes the same form as individual happiness, he will say that the city can engage in each kind of activity. But if you try and pin down which category he favours, organic or aggregative, he will say 'both': it all depends on the nature

---

[90] Another way of trying to identify the 'divine alien' of *Pol.* I 2, 1253a29 would be to point to 'heroic virtue', described at *NE* VII 1, 1145a18–29 as divine and the opposite of bestiality. See Saunders (1995) *ad loc.* But Aristotle is surely not referring to this kind of divine character in *Pol.* I 2, 1253a29, because in *NE* VII 1 he alludes to Hector as an example of heroic virtue, as well as referring to the way the Spartans called truly exemplary people 'divine' (cf. *Meno* 99d8–9). Such people were very much part of their societies, as archetypical leaders.

of the activity being identified with *eudaimonia*. If it is a highly structured activity, involving the close inter-relation of practical reason and the affective part, the type of happiness will be an organic, gestalt property; if the activity is theoretical contemplation, what else can it be except a number of citizens individually contemplating? This is not to deny that considerations of structure play any role in explaining why the state can be called 'contemplative': it is organised around the goal of promoting contemplation and those who contemplate are fully integrated members of the *polis*; and these are structural features. However, the activity of contemplation, when it occurs, does not itself involve the kind of structure we have found in morally virtuous activities. Contemplation by individual citizens is not co-ordinated and inter-related in the same way.

So, in the end, there is no reason why Aristotle cannot embrace both organic and aggregative accounts given the complexity of his views about *eudaimonia* (specifically that it comes in two forms). This means that contemplation is intrinsically good for the state, and this value is realised when a number of citizens engage in the activity, not as aliens but as fully fledged members of the state.

3.3 Appendix: The Aims of the State in *Pol.* III 6

In Section 3.2.3, I argued in favour of the organic interpretation of secondary *eudaimonia*. But we should discuss what has seemed to some to be a problem with this view. In Section 3.2.1, we listed four texts from the *Politics* that have been used to support the aggregative view. We can safely say that two of them are clearly compatible with the organic view: II 5, 1264b15–24 and VII 13, 1332a32–4, which merely imply in some (unstated) way that civic *eudaimonia* requires the *eudaimonia* of some citizens. But the other two (1323a14–19 and 1324a23–5) might seem more problematic, because they could be taken as implying a more direct connection between the aims of the legislator and individual happiness. Consider again *Pol.* VII 2, 1324a23–5:

> It is evident that the best constitution is that in which every person, whoever he is, can act best and live happily.

Martha Nussbaum, who supports the organic view for other passages in the *Politics*, thinks this text entails an aggregative (or as she puts it, a 'distributive') account of civic *eudaimonia*. The implicit argument here is that the best constitution aims at civic happiness; but, since it aims at the happiness of each individual citizen, civic happiness must be understood as aggregate of individual happiness. For this reason, she thinks that Aristotle confusingly embraces both the organic and aggregative views of civic happiness.[91]

Now, perhaps organic interpreters can dig in their heals: the best constitution aims at organic happiness; this is maximised when each citizen is happy (for the reasons given in Section 3.2.3); hence the maximally happy state will indeed be one in which 'every person, whoever he is, can act best and live happily'. But I think there is another way of accommodating this text (and the companion text quoted above, VII 1, 1323a14–19). We can see this by turning to a passage in *Pol.* III 6 where Aristotle talks directly about the purpose of the state:

> (1) First, then, we should state (a) our assumption about what end the city is constituted for, and (b) how many types of rule are concerned with human beings and with community of life. (2a) In our first discussions, when we determined the features of rule over households and over slaves, we also said that a human being is by nature a political animal. That is why, even when they have no need of mutual help, they still desire to live together; (2b) nevertheless, mutual interest also brings them together, to the extent that it contributes something to living nobly for each person. (3) Living nobly, then, most of all is the goal [of a city] for all in common and separately.[92]

I have numbered the different sections of this passage to bring out its structure. In (1) he sets out the two questions that he intends to answer, and the rest of the quote is his answer to the first (1a). (3) States the actual answer, while (2a) and (2b) state the reasoning that supports it.

The first of these premises, (2a), refers to *Pol.* I 2, with its famous claim that human beings are by nature political animals (1253a2–3). The claim here in III 6 seems to be that, because people are political animals, they seek to live together not only when they need help. There is an impulse in us that drives us to live together, even when we do not have to do so to meet our needs.[93] This then cues a discrete point (2b): nevertheless (οὐ μὴν ἀλλὰ) people also come together to seek mutual advantage for achieving their own ends, here specified as living the noble life (ζῆν καλῶς), that is, *eudaimonia* in Aristotle's sense. Putting these two points together, we can see that Aristotle is distinguishing two rationales behind the state's existence.[94]

---

[91] Nussbaum (1988) 146–50 and 158–60. See above n. 68. Morrison (2017) 22–24 raises a related problem: that Aristotle proposes an organic view of civic happiness, but an aggregative view of the common good, thereby seeming to undermine the coherence of his overall theory.

[92] 1278b15–24, trans. Irwin and Fine (1995) modified.

[93] Cf. I 2, 1253a29–30 with Barker (1946) 7 and 111.

[94] There is a third rationale, which is mentioned after the quoted passage: the state can be seen as providing for mere survival (1278b24–30). This is not generally Aristotle's favoured approach, but he thinks it worth mentioning as an appendix.

Now turn to (3): 'living nobly, then, most of all is the goal [of a city] for all in common and separately'.[95] Aristotle does not say explicitly to what or whom the end belongs (hence my use of square brackets). But it must be the city: that is the question he has been attempting to answer in (1a). Yet some translate the sentence as if the end, viz. noble action, is the end of human life, both when lived in a society and when lived individually.[96] But what he must be saying is that living nobly is the end *of the state* – for everyone in common or for individuals taken separately. In other words, the state exists to promote *eudaimonia* at two levels, for the citizens as a collective and for them as individuals.

These two levels, distinguished in (3), correspond to the two different rationales given for the existence of the state in (2). This is obvious in the case of (2b), which prepares the ground for saying that the state facilitates *eudaimonia* for the citizens as individuals. But I also think that (2a) helps explain what he means when he talks in (3) of the state's goal as living nobly 'for all in common'. To see this, we need to take a step back and ask why (2a) refers back to his famous claim from *Pol.* I 2 than human beings are political animals.

As expressed in *Pol.* I 2, this claim is intimately bound up with the thesis that the *polis* is prior to the individual, the thesis that we mentioned in Section 3.2.2, with its analogy between the state and a living body. The claim that human beings are political animals is stated both before and after this analogy (cf. 1253a1–18 and 27–39). So, to do justice to the fact that they are so closely related, we need to read them in the light of each other. This is not difficult to do: in saying that humans are by nature political animals, he means that it is part of their nature to live with others, specifically to form a part of a larger community that has a *telos* of its own; to serve a corporate goal. This is the desire to which (2a) refers. By contrast, (2b) points to the way the state can support a citizen's desire to achieve individual *eudaimonia*.

The upshot of this is that Aristotle can perfectly well maintain an organic conception of civic happiness, while claiming that the state also exists to promote individual happiness.

4 The Extent of Contemplation in Aristotle's Ideal State

4.1 Introduction

How many citizens would be expected to engage in contemplation in the ideal state? For Plato, the answer is clear. He is quite explicit that the class of philosopher-rulers is very small (*Rep.* IV 442c4). While somewhat bleak, this

---

[95] μάλιστα μὲν οὖν τοῦτ᾽ ἐστὶ τέλος, καὶ κοινῇ πᾶσι καὶ χωρίς.

[96] See e.g. Robinson (1995), Reeve (1998) and Morrison (2017) 23.

approach creates no tensions within his theory: the contemplation of the phil-osopher-rulers is needed to ensure the unity of the state, and the fact that the number of contemplators is very small does not undermine this goal.

For Aristotle, things are less straightforward. On one hand, he aspires to promote happiness as far as possible within the state. His pronouncements on promoting individual happiness are bold: 'it is evident that the form of govern-ment is best in which every person, whoever he is, can act best and live happily' (VII 2, 1324a23–5).[97] Since contemplation represents supreme happiness (*NE* X 7–8), it is an activity he should be especially keen to maximise. On the other hand, he is often thought to identify contemplation with a highly specialised discipline, the study of the divine, the 'highest' objects in the cosmos. Here are two passages from *NE* VI 7 to that effect:

> Therefore wisdom (*sophia*) must be intuitive reason (*nous*) combined with knowledge (*epistēmē*) – knowledge of the highest objects which has received as it were its proper completion. Of the highest objects, we say; for it would be strange to think that the art of politics, or practical wisdom, is the best knowledge, since a human being is not the best thing in the world. (1141a18–22)

> But if the argument be that humans are the best of the animals, this makes no difference; for there are other things much more divine in their nature even than humans, e.g., most conspicuously, the bodies of which the heavens are framed. From what has been said it is plain, then, that wisdom is knowledge combined with intuitive reason of the things that are highest by nature. (1141a33 b3)

Other passages in the *NE* have been taken to suggest a similarly demanding view of contemplation.[98] Scholars have identified this with Aristotle's own metaphysical theology or 'first philosophy'. If the *Metaphysics* is anything to go by, this sort of study would start with empirical observation of natural phenomena along with a survey of his predecessors' views on the relevant topics, and then develop into an increasingly abstract investigation into sub-stance, essence, and form, culminating in contemplation of the unmoved mover. If this is an accurate account of what is required for contemplation, Aristotle cannot reasonably expect more than a handful of citizens to engage in it.

How serious is this problem? Richard Kraut implies that it would generate an 'intolerable paradox' if Aristotle were to insist that, 'in the best city, where people are as happy as possible, at most a few will achieve the perfect happiness that Aristotle equates with philosophical contemplation'.[99] In reply, some might say that there is no paradox here, let alone an intolerable one. In the ideal state,

---

[97] See also VII 1, 1323a14–19.
[98] X 7, 1177a12–18 and 1177b31–1178a2; X 8, 1178b7–32 and 1179a22–32.
[99] Kraut (2002) 198.

the aim is indeed to make people as happy as possible, but the qualification 'as possible' might mean that they achieve only as much happiness as their natural capacities allow. For most people, this does not involve immersion in meta-physical theology. Nonetheless, given the right educational programme, they can still aspire to a life that is happiest in a 'secondary degree', the life of moral virtue and practical reason (*NE* X 8, 1178a9–20). Meanwhile, those few who possess the capacity for contemplation will be enabled to fulfil it. At the level of the individual, everyone will achieve as much happiness as is possible – for them.[100]

There is no formal contradiction in Aristotle's position, even if he really does limit the scope of contemplation to metaphysical theology. But perhaps there is still a tension, if not a paradox. In his discussion of the ideal state at *Pol.* VII 14–15, he argues that its happiness requires leisure, where the necessities of life have been met and its citizens are free from labour of various kinds. But this in turn raises the question of what they are meant to do with such leisure: safe from enemy attack and well provided with external goods, how are they to use their time?

It would certainly not be enough for them to occupy themselves with pleasure and amusement; they need to engage in activity of some kind. Specifically, they need to engage in *praxis*, without which there can be no *eudaimonia*. By *praxis* I mean an activity that has its end in itself, a noble activity. Just and temperate actions have a dual role to play here. They help secure leisure by producing health and civic concord respectively. But in so far as they do this, they count as 'production', *poiēsis*, Aristotle's term for action done for an end beyond itself. They are also instrumentally necessary for maintaining leisure: abundance brings dangers of its own, which justice and temperance are well-suited to address.[101] At the same time, being noble, they are choiceworthy in themselves; as such they also count as examples of *praxis*. This means that engaging in, for example, justice – attending courts and assemblies – also counts as using leisure to engage in *eupraxia* and hence to achieve *eudaimonia*. By contrast, contem-plation has no end outside of itself. It is pure *praxis*, never at the same time *poiēsis*. It never helps us achieve or maintain the conditions of leisure; it is just what we use leisure for. Hence, it provides the perfect answer to the question of how to spend our leisure-time and ensure that it leads to *eudaimonia*.

In fact, Aristotle goes further than this, claiming that philosophy is necessary for happiness (1334a23 and 32), and he makes no attempt to whittle this down by allowing most citizens to make do with justice and temperance (thereby securing for themselves a life of secondary happiness). True, at one point he

---

[100] According to Roochnik (2008) 733–35, Aristotle mentions philosophy and contemplation in the *Politics* to show us the absolute ideal, unrealizable for most people.
[101] VII 15, 1334a11–36. On this, see Kraut (1997) 144.

does (rather obliquely) let slip that not everyone is capable of contemplation (VII 14, 1333a27–9), but if he really thought that large swathes of the population are barred from the activity, why is there no mention of the fact?

This, of course, is only an argument from silence; as such, it may cut little ice with those who see no problem in Aristotle's thought, not even a tension. In what follows, however, I shall work on the assumption that there is a *prima facie* tension in Aristotle's philosophy, and seek to resolve it. I shall do this by arguing that Aristotle did not limit intellectual contemplation to metaphysical theology. Contemplation covers a broader range of intellectual activity, accessible to a larger swathe of the citizenry than is usually thought.

4.2 Contemplation and Culture

Before pursuing this solution, I wish to review a very different attempt to expand the range of contemplation in Aristotle's ideal state. There is a view in the literature, going back to Friedrich Solmsen in the 1960s, that the virtue termed *philosophia* in *Pol.* VII 15 and the corresponding activity of contemplation should not be understood in the intellectualist way presented in the *NE*.[102] Solmsen argued that, in the *Politics*, Aristotle has in mind cultural engagement, particularly in *mousikē*, the combination of music and poetry. When he suggested the idea, he pointed to the way that the rest of the *Politics* proceeds: in VII 13–15, Aristotle talks about the way the legislator is going to promote his citizens' correct use of leisure and plan their education accordingly. Even though he uses the term *philosophia* to describe the virtue that is to be actualised in leisure, when he goes on to describe the educational programme in book VIII, he is almost exclusively concerned with *mousikē*.[103] If contemplation involves engagement in the arts, especially music and poetry, it is easy to see how most citizens can be expected to participate in it.[104]

Solmsen's view has proved controversial.[105] One objection to his reading stems from its assumption that Aristotle ever uses the word *philosophia* to refer

---

[102] Solmsen (1964) 218. More recently the interpretation has been espoused by Lord (1982) 199–202 and, in a modified form, by Kraut (1997) 139–40 and (2002) 201–202.

[103] Solmsen (1964) 214–16.

[104] Note how this interpretation decouples the *Politics* from the *NE*: Solmsen does not deny that the *NE* takes a narrowly intellectual view of contemplation; but he thinks Aristotle uses a different conception of *philosophia* and contemplation in the *Politics*, which is the text that seems to suggest that contemplation should be practised widely among the citizens.

[105] For two lengthy critiques, see Depew (1991) and Koeplin (2009). In response to Solmsen's argument that the educational programme of VIII is almost exclusively taken up with *mousikē*, Koeplin (2009) 124–5 rightly points out: 'the *Politics* as we know it is almost certainly incomplete. The text contains a whole series of unfulfilled promises.' So the absence of a discussion of intellectual contemplation in *Pol.* VIII is not a particularly strong argument in Solmsen's favour.

to *mousikē* and literary culture elsewhere. Certainly, it is a term with a very broad range, but it may always refer to some sort of intellectual pursuit. Whether it can be even broader than this and refer to artistic or cultural pursuits is far from clear, although it cannot be ruled out. Aristotle sometimes defines *philosophia* very narrowly: in *Met.* XII 8 1073b4, it is used in its most restrictive sense, to refer only to 'first philosophy' (metaphysical theology) and is distinguished from the mathematical sciences. But he also uses it to cover intellectual interests more generally. *Metaphysics* VI 1 groups together different theoretical disciplines as a species of *philosophia*, implying that practical disciplines could also count.[106] But although it a very broad term, the crucial question is whether its meaning extends beyond intellectual culture. I can see no examples where the term obviously refers to cultural, for example, literary, pursuits. One advocate for Solmsen's view, Carnes Lord, points to a passage in *Pol.* II 5, which talks of improving the citizens of a state 'by habits, philosophy and laws' (1263b39–40). He claims that 'philosophy' here refers to a society's 'traditional culture', especially its 'literary culture'.[107] But we cannot be sure of this; the term might mean intellectual culture.[108] One might make the weaker claim merely that the love of artistic culture is similar to philosophy. In *Poetics* 9, 1451b5–7, Aristotle claims that poetry is more philosophical than history because it deals more with the universal.[109] But this still falls short of identifying literary culture as a form of *philosophia*.[110] In general, the evidence for taking the term *philosophia* to refer to artistic culture is weak.

Solmsen's view also runs into difficulties when we look at the flow of argument in *Pol.* VII 13–15. In this passage, Aristotle mentions *philosophia* as part of a discussion about what virtues the statesman needs to cultivate among his citizens. *Philosophia* appears alongside courage, justice and temperance as the cluster of virtues required in the ideal state (VII 15). He also insists that the statesman should rank these virtues, depending on whether they are inferior or superior, and on whether they have instrumental or intrinsic value. He maps these virtues and their associated activities onto the distinction

---

[106] See also the phrase 'the philosophy of human affairs' in *NE* X, 9 1181b15, used as a description of his ethical and political inquiries.

[107] Lord (1982) 200.   [108] As Newman (1887) II 255 argues.

[109] Kraut (2002) 202 n. 22. See also *Met.* I 2, 982b18–20, which says that the lover of myth (*philomuthos*) is a *philosophos* is some sense: both exhibit an attitude of wonder. (However, Aristotle is unlikely to be stressing the literary uses or dimensions of myth; presumably he is thinking of myths as the precursors to scientific inquiry.)

[110] See Moore (2019) 350. Lord (1982) 199 n. 21 and Kraut (2002) 198 n.12 also cite Pericles' boast in Thucydides (II 40.1) that 'we philosophise without softness' (II 40.1), taking this to refer to the Athenians' cultural achievements. But just before this phrase Pericles asserts, 'we love beauty without extravagance'. Surely this refers to their cultural pursuits, leaving the reference to philosophy to cover intellectual interests.

between leisurely and non-leisurely activities: courage is associated with purely non-leisurely activity, temperate and just activities are both leisurely and non-leisurely, while *philosophia* is purely leisurely.

But these are not the only considerations that the statesman has to bear in mind when thinking about the virtues and their corresponding activities. He also needs to take account of moral psychology. In VII 14, 1333a16–27, Aristotle sets out the division of the soul familiar to us from *NE* I 13, between the rational and affective parts, and, within the rational, between practical and theoretical reasoning. Immediately after distinguishing these three soul parts, he says that we can also distinguish different activities corresponding to them, adding:

> The actions of the naturally better part are to be preferred by those who have it in their power to attain to two out of the three or to all, for that is always to everyone the most choiceworthy which is the highest attainable by them. (1333a27–30)

It is at this point that he introduces the distinction between work and leisure as one criterion for ranking different virtues (and their corresponding activities). But shortly afterwards, he returns to the division of the soul to say that the statesman should always keep in mind the distinctions between the different parts of the soul (1333a38–9). Aristotle's insistence that the statesman should bear in mind the different parts of the soul – including theoretical reason – is a major stumbling block for Solmsen's view. By understanding *philosophia* in terms of cultural engagement rather than intellectual contemplation, he makes the theoretical part of the psychological distinction completely irrelevant to the argument, despite Aristotle's explicit instruction to the contrary. (Engagement in *mousikē* is not an activity of the theoretical part, which is solely concerned with eternal and unchanging truths.)

Furthermore, when we ask ourselves how the statesman will take account of the psychological distinctions in his law-making, the obvious answer is to do precisely what Solmsen tell us to avoid: to import the theory set out in the *NE*. The highest part of the soul is theoretical reason; the virtue of that part is *philosophia*, and its activity is also purely leisurely, having no goal beyond itself. On this account, it is easy to see how the distinction between parts of the soul and between work and leisure converge, as Aristotle expects them to.

4.3 The Extent of Intellectual Contemplation

Let me now pursue my own way of extending the scope of contemplation, which will proceed by broadening the range of what counts as a theoretical science and so establishing that the theoretical intellect operates over a wide terrain, not just metaphysical theology. At certain points in the *Metaphysics*, Aristotle makes a three-fold division among theoretical sciences:

There must, then, be three theoretical philosophies, mathematics, natural science, and what we may call theology, since it is obvious that if the divine is present anywhere, it is present in things of this sort.[111] And the highest science must deal with the highest genus. Thus, while the theoretical sciences are more to be desired than the other sciences, this is more to be desired than the other theoretical sciences. (*Met*. VI 1, 1026a18–23)

But since there is one kind of thinker who is above even the natural scientist (for nature is only one particular genus of being), the discussion of these truths also will belong to him whose inquiry is universal and deals with primary substance. Natural science is also a kind of wisdom (*sophia*), but it is not the first kind. (*Met*. IV 3, 1005a33–b2)

Philosophy does not inquire about particular subjects in so far as each of them has some attribute or other, but speculates about being, in so far as each particular thing is. Natural science is in the same position as mathematics; for natural science studies the attributes and the principles of the things that are, *qua* moving and not *qua* being (whereas the primary science, we have said, deals with these, only in so far as the underlying subjects are existent, and not in virtue of any other character); and so both natural science and mathematics must be classed as parts of wisdom. (*Met*. XI 4, 1061b25–33)

These texts make it clear that Aristotle has a broad understanding of theoretical (contemplative) science, one that embraces not only theology (metaphysics), but also natural science and mathematics. The highest form of contemplation is concerned with first causes; it is theological in nature. But those engaged in mathematics or natural science can still be said to contemplate, because they are activating the theoretical part of their intellect. And the crucial point for our purposes is that both these species of *sophia* are more accessible than metaphysical theology – as I shall now attempt to show.

This can easily be seen on the case of one of the natural sciences, biology. In the *Parts of Animals* 1 5, Aristotle compares biology with 'first philosophy' (i.e. metaphysical theology):

We are better equipped to acquire knowledge about the perishable plants and animals because they grow beside us: much can be learned about each existing kind if one is willing to take sufficient pains. . . . Also, because they are closer to us and belong more to our nature, they have their own compensations in comparison with the philosophy concerned with the divine things.[112]

---

[111] 'Things of this sort' presumably refers to 1026a16: things that are 'separable and immovable'.
[112] I 5, 645a12–17, trans. Balme (1992). In *NE* VI 8, 1141a12–18, Aristotle states that mathematics is more accessible than first philosophy or natural science to the young. I discuss this passage in Section 4.4.1.

A similar point can be made about mathematics. Think for a moment of the most famous textbook in geometry, Euclid's *Elements*, written around 300 BC and used widely in schools and colleges right up until the nineteenth century (and, in some cases, beyond): the collection of proofs that deduces a large number of propositions from a relatively small set of principles. Euclid's work conforms, at least in general terms, to Aristotle's conception of a science set out in the *Posterior Analytics*. The whole work operates at a level of abstraction that could satisfy Aristotle's requirement of studying what is necessary and unvarying. Of course, there is a great deal of uncertainty and controversy as to how closely Euclid's system matched the ideal Aristotle sets out in the *Posterior Analytics*.[113] Since Euclid post-dates Aristotle, we have to be wary of anachronism. But some of the theorems Aristotle mentions as examples in the work appear as fully worked out proofs in Euclid.[114] So it is highly likely that the level of difficulty that would be experienced by someone working through the proofs in an Aristotelian mathematics would be very similar to the level required by Euclid. And as is well, known, this level has been found to be widely attainable in schools and colleges down the centuries. So, in terms of accessibility, mathematics scores high, certainly higher than metaphysical theology.

4.4 Divinity and Contemplation in the *Nicomachean Ethics*

To solve the problem about the narrowness of contemplation, I have argued that Aristotle has a broad notion, embracing not only metaphysical theology, but also mathematics and natural science. But is this response compatible with those texts that associate contemplation with the study of the divine? All these texts, it should be said, come from the *NE*. The *Politics* presents no difficulty in this respect because it does not mention divinity at all.[115] So in this section, we shall examine the relevant passages from *NE* VI and X that link contemplation to the study of the divine and see whether they really do exclude mathematics and biology from the realm of contemplation.

---

[113] For an overview of the debate and the different positions that have been taken up, see McKirahan (1992) 135–36, with references to Heath (1925) I 117, Lee (1935), Solmsen (1975) 126–28 and Szabó (1978).

[114] *An. Po.* I 5, 74a8–9 and 17–25 = Euclid V 16 (the general theory of proportion); *An. Po.* I 7, 75b13 = Euclid IX 4; *An. Po.* II 11, 94a24 = Euclid III 31. Compare also the proof mentioned in *Met.* IX 1051a21–6 with Euclid I 32 (cf. *An. Po.* I 1, 71a17–20). Both Aristotle and Euclid were drawing on theorems discovered by earlier mathematicians, for example, Theudius, Archytas and Theaetetus, hence the overlap.

[115] On Aristotle's reticence about the divine aspects of contemplation in the *Politics*, see Kraut (1997) 75–76. There is a reference to god's happiness in *Pol.* VII 1, 1323b24–6, but this is not a specific reference to the activity of contemplation, merely to the fact that god is happy through his own nature, not through external goods. On this passage, see Roochnik (2008) 727–28.

4.4.1 Sophia in NE VI

Sophia is defined in this chapter as the combination of *nous* and *epistēmē*, that is, as the combined understanding of principles of and proofs. As we saw in Section 4.1, at two points, 1141a18–22 and 1141a 33–b3, Aristotle implies that it has a narrow focus, stating that it is concerned with the 'worthiest' objects, those out of which the universe is composed. There is a reference to divinity in the second of these passages, at 1141a 34. A few lines later, at 1141b7, he also implies that the objects of *sophia* are 'divine' (*daimonia*). This sounds like a reference to first philosophy, or theology, which studies the prime mover.

But there are reasons to think he also has a broader conception of *sophia* in mind here and that any science that combines knowledge of both principles and proofs would count as *sophia*. Earlier, when discussing one of the components of *sophia* in VI 3, *epistēmē*, he referred to his *Analytics*, using terminology from its description of demonstrative science. Presumably, his conception of *epistēmē* has not changed when he comes to discuss *sophia* in VI 7, just a few pages later. But the *An. Po.* clearly assumes that mathematics counts as a paradigm demonstrative science (this is evident from the number of mathematical examples used). So, given the link with the *An. Po.* made in *NE* VI 3, we would expect *sophia* in VI 7 to include mathematics. This is confirmed by an example of the type of property that *sophia* might study: straightness (1141a23).[116] So the account of *sophia* in *NE* VI 7 seems to point in two directions. I think the best way of dealing with this is to say that, like the term *philosophia*,[117] *sophia* can have narrow and broad senses: *sophia* in the strict sense is theology, but other sciences count as *sophia* in a looser sense (cf. *Met.* IV 3, 1005b1–2).

Support for this point can be found in the following chapter, VI 8. As part of his discussion of political *phronēsis*, Aristotle stresses the need for experience. He then draws a contrast between *phronēsis* and mathematics:

> What has been said is confirmed by the fact that, while the young become geometricians and mathematicians and wise (*sophoi*) in matters like these, it is thought that a young person of *phronēsis* cannot be found. The cause is that such *phronēsis* is concerned not only with universals but with particulars, which become familiar from experience, but a young person has no experience, for it is length of time that gives experience; indeed one might ask this question too, why a child may become a mathematician, but not wise (*sophos*) or a natural scientist. It is because the objects of mathematics exist by abstraction, while the first principles of these other subjects come from experience. (VI 8, 1142a11–19)

---

[116] At the same point, he also refers to whiteness, implying that the science concerned with colour, like his own work on perceptibles, falls under the ambit of *sophia*.

[117] See *Met.* VI 1, 1026a18–19, quoted Section in 4.3, where *philosophia* is used to refer to theology, mathematics or natural science.

At first sight, this may appear confusing: Aristotle begins by allowing that the young can be wise (*sophoi*, a13) but then seems to withdraw the claim (17–18). But we can use some of the points we have already made to dispel any appearance of contradiction. What Aristotle allows to the young is possession of *sophia* in a qualified sense, 'in matters like these', that is, mathematics. What he denies them is *sophia* is the unqualified sense, 'first philosophy', knowledge of the divine. On his view, abstract as this science may be, it still requires (initially) immersion in sense experience: we are discovering the ultimate causes of the whole cosmos.[118]

4.4.2 Divinity and Contemplation in NE X 7–8

The link between contemplation and divinity is made right at the start of X 7:

> If *eudaimonia* is activity in accordance with virtue, it is reasonable that it should be in accordance with the highest virtue; and this will be that of the best thing in us. Whether it be intellect or something else that is this element which is thought to be our natural ruler and guide and to take thought of things beautiful (*kalōn*) and divine, whether it be itself also divine or only the most divine element in us, the activity of this in accordance with its proper virtue will be perfect *eudaimonia*. That this activity is contemplative we have already said. (X 7, 1177a12–18)

This confidently asserts that perfect happiness consists in the activity of the best thing in us (cf. *NE* I 7, 1098a17–18). Aristotle appears uncertain about whether this faculty is actually divine or merely the most godlike thing in us, though he does assert that this element is concerned with things that are beautiful and divine. So our problem is that, even if there is a form of contemplation that is not concerned with the divine, this activity will not constitute happiness of the kind at issue here.

However, this objection can be met. Aristotle's argument here does not rely on the claim that contemplation is only of divine objects. It is premised instead on the claim that perfect *eudaimonia* is the activity of the best thing in us. He then points to a faculty within us that is capable of apprehending things that are 'divine and beautiful'. Since it has this capability, it must be the best thing in us. Hence the activity of this faculty must be perfect happiness. This does not imply that, whenever we use this faculty, we are contemplating divine things; merely that we are using a faculty capable of doing so. In other words, there is a difference between claiming (a) contemplation involves thinking about divine objects and (b) contemplation involves using a faculty that is capable of

---

[118] Mathematics, *sophia* and physical science are being treated in *NE* VI 8 as they were in the three passages we quoted from the *Metaphysics* in Section 4.3: see Burnet (1900) 272–73.

thinking about divine objects. Since only (b) is stated here, it is possible for there to be a form of contemplation that does not study divine objects. Doubtless, this kind of activity would be even more valuable if we mastered theology, but even if we are doing geometry or biology, we are still actualising the best faculty in us.

There are two further arguments for the primacy of contemplation based on considerations about divinity in book X, both in chapter 8. In the first, 1178b7–32, Aristotle argues that *eudaimonia* is something we associate especially with the gods. But if it involves activity of some kind, what activity will they be engaged in? He rejects moral activity, claiming that it is absurd to think of the gods engaging in the kind of acts associated with courage, justice and generosity (e.g. warfare and the exchange of contracts); the only activity left for them is contemplation. He concludes, 'and of human activities, therefore, that which is most akin (συγγενεστάτη) to this must, most of all, be the nature of happiness' (1178b23). The other divinity-based argument for the primacy of contemplation comes at the end of the chapter (1179a22–32). Appealing to common intuitions about the interest the gods take in us, he argues that they love most whatever is best and most akin (συγγενεστάτῳ) to them. Human beings who value contemplative reason will therefore be most loved by the gods and hence benefited by them.

In these two arguments, he stresses the link between divinity and contemplation, but he does not go as far as to identify contemplation with the study of the divine. True, the gods will study the worthiest objects when they contemplate, and we know that in *Met*. XII 9 the unmoved mover contemplates himself (1074b21–35). But for the arguments in *NE* X 8 to work, they only need to assume that human contemplation is *similar* to divine activity. Would Aristotle think this true of mathematics and natural science?

The idea that other forms of theoretical science bear a similarity to theology can be found elsewhere in the corpus. Consider the case of biology. In a famous chapter towards the beginning of the *Parts of Animals* (cited in Section 4.3), Aristotle defends the study of biology, even though it is not as elevated as theology. There is beauty and order in the natural world, and this is not to be spurned. In a famous aside, he recalls an anecdote about Heraclitus:

> For in all natural things there is something wonderful. And just as Heraclitus is said to have spoken to the visitors, who were wanting to meet him but stopped as they were approaching when they saw him warming himself at the oven – he kept telling them to come in and not worry, 'for there are gods here too' – so we should approach the inquiry about each animal without aversion, knowing that in all of them there is something natural and beautiful.[119]

---

[119] I 5, 645a17–23, trans. Balme (1992).

Even if biology is not literally the study of the divine, it studies something beautiful and ordered, which has some similarity with the divine. And recall that, at the beginning of *NE* X 7, Aristotle said that the supreme element in us studies what is beautiful as well as divine (1177a15).

As far as I know, Aristotle never explicitly talks of mathematics as being similar to the divine. But since he talks of our highest faculty as something capable of grasping things that are beautiful as well as divine, we should take note of the following passage, where he associates mathematics with beauty and order:

> Now since the good and the beautiful are different (for the former always implies conduct as its subject, while the beautiful is found also in motionless things), those who assert that the mathematical sciences say nothing of the beautiful or the good are in error. . . . The chief forms of beauty are order and symmetry and definiteness, which the mathematical sciences demonstrate in a special degree. And since these (e.g. order and definiteness) are obviously causes of many things, evidently these sciences must treat this sort of cause also (i.e. the beautiful) as in some sense a cause. (*Met.* XIII 3, 1078a31–b5)

It is also worth noting that one form of mathematics, astronomy, has a particular proximity to theology, or first philosophy. Aristotle makes the point when introducing astronomy into his argument about prime movers at *Met.* XII 8, 1073b5–8.

4.5 Objections and Replies

I have argued that Aristotle has a broad notion of contemplation, with three species, all of which contribute to primary *eudaimonia*, the kind that is ranked over the life of *phronēsis* and moral virtue in *NE* X 7–8. This is true, even though one of them, the exercise of *sophia* in its unqualified sense, counts as the absolute gold standard.[120] My purpose all along has been to argue for an understanding of contemplation that can be practised by a large number of citizens. But it could be objected that this provides only a limited solution to the original problem. Aristotle still seems to expect that his citizens will become experts in natural science or mathematics. Yet this seems a rather meagre extension: the number of professional mathematicians and natural scientists is still small.

By way of a quick response, we might remind ourselves that Euclid's *Elements* formed part of the school and college curriculum for many centuries. So perhaps Aristotle is not being unrealistic (assuming, once again, that his conception of mathematics was at a similar level of difficulty). But perhaps this is a little naïve: did adolescents and college students really master all the books of Euclid, immersing themselves in all the proofs contained therein? Isn't it

---

[120] On my view, not only does *eudaimonia* split into primary and secondary types; within the primary there are grades of perfection.

more likely that they had only a partial understanding and that a lot of the time students relied on rote-memorising rather than diligently studying the logical relationships between each step of each proof?[121]

To respond to this objection, we need to consider a further way of broadening the scope of contemplation, beyond saying that there are other types of *sophia* than metaphysical theology. This involves thinking about the threshold at which contemplation can be said to start. Within the case of mathematics, for example, there are degrees of participation in *theōria*. There is the professional mathematician, of course, but at the other end of the spectrum consider a student – in our terms, either at high school or in the first year at university – who has been studying geometry. What might this involve? I have already referred to Aristotle's *Posterior Analytics,* which presents a model to which any science should conform, a tightly unified system of principles and proofs. Although deeply influenced by what was the most successful example in his day, mathematics, he thought the same pattern of scientific demonstration could be applied to other disciplines, such as biology. But because mathematics (including arithmetic and geometry) was so much at the forefront of his mind, most of his examples of proof are mathematical. The expert will have grasped the set of principles or axioms and then seen how a large number of theorems can be derived from them. They will have achieved a synoptic mastery of the whole system.

But consider someone who has only grasped a part of the discipline: they have studied a small number of proofs, but at least in these cases they are able to start with the first principles and see how these or some of them, taken together, imply the theorem in question. (They are not relying on rote-learning.) Having studied this far, they are able to stand back and contemplate what they have learnt. What part of their soul, according to Aristotle, is operative here? It has to be the theoretical subdivision of the rational part. It is not as if students use practical reason or *technē* in doing geometry, while professors use theoretical intellect. Such a student has already passed the threshold into contemplation.[122] So my reply to the objection is that one is still actualising theoretical reason, even if one has only a partial understanding of geometry or of any of the mathematical or natural sciences.

---

[121] On the danger of rote-learning Euclidean geometry, see Moktefi (2011) 324–25.

[122] Also relevant here is Aristotle's distinction between a professional scientist and someone with a more generalised form of knowledge, but who can still follow what they are saying. See *NE* I 3, 1095a1–2 and *Parts of Animals* I 1, 639a4–15 with Irwin (1988) 27–29, Kraut (1997) 140, Reeve (1998) 248–49 and Leunissen (2015) 227–28. In these texts, Aristotle is talking about something slightly different from the type of student I have been discussing. He has in mind a person of general education who can judge whether a treatise is following the right methods, according to the appropriate level of precision. But if Aristotle recognises that someone can have this general level of acquaintance in contrast to a specialised knowledge, he should allow that a relatively wide circle of people can contemplate, even if not at the level of the expert.

Nonetheless, this response gives rise to yet another objection. Partial understanding does not constitute *sophia*, the virtue of the theoretical intellect (even qualified forms of *sophia*, such as mathematics or natural science). Hence, whatever activity one engages in cannot count as activity in accordance with virtue; as such, it cannot be *eudaimonia*. So would Aristotle actually have recommended that the citizens engage in it?

In response, consider the following passage from *NE* X 7:

> But we must not follow those who advise us, being human, to think of human things, and, being mortal, of mortal things, but must, so far as we can, make ourselves immortal, and strain every nerve to live in accordance with the best thing in us; for even if it be small in bulk, much more does it in power and worth surpass everything. (1177b31–1178a2)

This passage comes towards the end of the chapter, after Aristotle has set out a series of arguments in favour of pursuing intellectual contemplation. Here he mentions an objection that could be raised against him, but then provides a response. When he talks of intellect being 'small in bulk' he is probably saying that the efforts of even the greatest human thinker are puny compared to the activity of the unmoved mover. His point is that this difference, however great, is no reason not to contemplate to the best of one's ability. But, as a general point, this should apply also to anyone who has at least some ability to contemplate. Consider an adolescent (or a citizen heavily burdened with political tasks) who can follow a few proofs but is tempted to abandon the activity because their efforts seem puny compared to a professional. The argument Aristotle advances above forbids this type of defeatism as much as it forbids a professional giving up in the realisation that another being (the unmoved mover) far surpasses them: just a small amount of contemplation possesses so much value that it is always worthwhile. As soon as one passes the threshold into contemplation, the value of what one is doing should override any temptation not to persevere.[123]

---

[123] A final point: at the end of Section 3.1.2, I raised the question of whether Aristotle would have modified his anti-instrumentalism about theoretical knowledge by conceding that some sciences have technological applications. In the light of what we have now concluded about the scope of contemplation, we can say that perfect contemplation, the activity of 'first philosophy', that is, metaphysical theology, does not have any instrumental application. But there can be other kinds of contemplation, less perfect forms, such as biology, and it would be implausible to deny the uses of such knowledge. Aristotle's view is most likely that, the more perfect the type of contemplation, the more it is pursued only for itself. Conversely, the further a discipline stands from the ideal, the more likely it is to have technological application. This is not surprising: such disciplines are 'closer to us', as he puts it – more rooted in the material and the perceptible.

References

Ackrill, J. (1980) 'Aristotle on *eudaimonia*', in Rorty, 15–33.

Adam, J. (1963) *The Republic of Plato*. 2 Vols. 2nd ed. Cambridge.

Adamson, P. and Rapp, C. eds. (2021) *State and Nature: Studies in Ancient and Medieval Philosophy*. Berlin.

Annas, J. (1981) *An Introduction to Plato's Republic*. Oxford.

Apelt, O. trans. (1916) *Platon: Der Staat*. Leipzig.

Arends, J. (1988) *Die Einheit der Polis*. Leiden.

Baccou, R. trans. (1936) *Oeuvres complètes de Platon*. Vol. IV. Paris.

Balme, D. ed. (1992) *Aristotle, De Partibus Animalium I and De Generatione Animalium I (with passages from II 1–3)*. 2nd ed. Oxford.

Barker, E. (1946) *The Politics of Aristotle*. Oxford.

Barnes, J. ed. (1984) *The Complete Works of Aristotle*. 2 Vols. Princeton.

Barney, R., Brennan, T. and Brittain, C. eds. (2012) *Plato and the Divided Self*. Cambridge.

Bermon, E., Laurand, V. and Terrel, J. eds. (2017) *L'excellence Politique Chez Aristote*. Leuven.

Bodéüs, R. (1993) *The Political Dimension of Aristotle's Ethics* (*Le Philosophe et la Cité*), trans. Garrett J. Albany.

Bostock, D. (2000) *Aristotle's Ethics*. Oxford.

Broadie, S. (1991) *Ethics with Aristotle*. Oxford.

Broadie, S. and Rowe, C. eds. (2002) *Aristotle: Nicomachean Ethics*. Oxford.

Brown, L. (1998) 'How totalitarian is Plato's *Republic*?', in Ostenfeld, 13–27.

Burnet, J. ed. (1900) *The Ethics of Aristotle*. London.

Chambry, É. trans. (1959) *Platon, Oeuvres complètes: La République*. Paris.

Cooper, J. ed. (1997) *Plato, Complete Works*. Indianapolis.

Cooper, J. (2010) 'Political community and the highest good', in Lennox and Bolton, 212–64.

Cousin, V. trans. (1833) *Oeuvres de Platon*. Vol. IX. Paris.

Cross, R. and Woozley, A. (1964) *Plato's Republic*. London.

Curzer, H. (2020) Review of Matthew Walker, *Aristotle on the Uses of Contemplation. Polis* 37: 177–220.

Denniston, J. (1981) *The Greek Particles*. 2nd ed. Oxford.

Depew, D. (1991) 'Politics, music, and contemplation in Aristotle's ideal state', in Keyt and Miller, 346–80.

Deslauriers, M. and Destrée, P. eds. (2013) *The Cambridge Companion to Aristotle's Politics*. Cambridge.

Emlyn-Jones, C. and Preddy, W. trans. (2013) *Plato: The Republic*. 2 Vols. Cambridge.

Everson, S. ed. (1990) *Cambridge Companions to Ancient Thought I: Epistemology*. Cambridge.

Ferrari, G. ed. (2007) *The Cambridge Companion to Plato's Republic*. Cambridge.

Ferrari, G. and Griffith, T. trans. (2000) *Plato: The Republic*. Cambridge.

Fine, G. (1990) 'Knowledge and belief in *Republic* V–VII', in Everson, 85–115.

Fine, G. ed. (1999) *Plato II: Ethics, Politics, Religion and the Soul*. Oxford.

Fine, G. ed. (2008) *The Oxford Handbook of Plato*. Oxford.

Flood, R., Rice, A. and Wilson, R. eds. (2011) *Mathematics in Victorian Britain*. Oxford.

Frank, J. (2015) 'On *logos* and politics in Aristotle', in Lockwood and Samaras, 9–26.

Frede, D. (2013) 'The political character of Aristotle's ethics', in Deslauriers and Destrée, 14–37.

Garsten, B. (2013) 'Rhetoric and human separateness', *Polis* 30: 210–27.

Grube, G. (1974) *Plato: The Republic*. London.

Grube, G. (1997) *Plato: The Republic*. Rev. Reeve, C. D. C. in Cooper, 971–1223.

Harbin, K. (2019) Review of Walker (M. D.) *Aristotle on the Uses of Contemplation*. *Classical Review* 69: 405–407.

Hardie, W. (1980) *Aristotle's Ethical Theory*. 2nd ed. Oxford.

Harding, S. and Hintikka, M. eds. (1983) *Discovering Reality*. Dordrecht.

Heath, T. ed. (1925) *The Thirteen Books of Euclid's Elements*. 3 Vols. Cambridge.

Henry, D. and Nielsen, K. eds. (2015) *Bridging the Gap between Aristotle's Science and Ethics*. Cambridge.

Hirji, S. (2020) Review of Matthew D. Walker, *Aristotle on the Uses of Contemplation*. *Philosophical Review* 129: 465–68.

Irwin, T. (1988) *Aristotle's First Principles*. Oxford.

Irwin, T. (1995) *Plato's Ethics*. Oxford.

Irwin, T. (1999) '*Republic* 2: Questions about justice', in Fine, 164–85.

Irwin, T. and Fine, G. trans. (1995) *Aristotle: Selections*. Indianapolis.

Jowett, B. trans. (1984) *Aristotle's Politics*, in Barnes, II 1986–2129.

Jowett, B. and Campbell, L. eds. (1894) *Plato's Republic*. 3 Vols. Oxford.

Keyt, D. (1987) 'Three fundamental theorems in Aristotle's *Politics*', *Phronesis* 32: 54–79.

Keyt, D. and F. Miller, F. eds. (1991) *A Companion to Aristotle's Politics*. Oxford.

Koeplin, A. (2009) 'The *telos* of the citizen life: Music and philosophy in Aristotle's ideal *polis*', *Polis* 26: 116–32.

Kraut, R. ed. (1997) *Aristotle: Politics, Books VII and VIII*. Oxford.

Kraut, R. (1999) 'Return to the cave: *Republic* 519–521', in Fine, 235–54.

Kraut, R. (2002) *Aristotle: Political Philosophy*. Oxford.

Kraut, R. ed. (2006) *The Blackwell Guide to Aristotle's Nicomachean Ethics*. Oxford.

Kullman, W. (1991) 'Man as a political animal in Aristotle', in Keyt and Miller, 94–117.

Lee, H. (1935) 'Geometrical method and Aristotle's account of first principles', *Classical Quarterly* 29: 113–24.

Lee, D. (1974) *Plato: The Republic*. 2nd ed. London.

Lennox, J. and Bolton, R. eds. (2010) *Being, Nature, and Life in Aristotle*. Cambridge.

Leunissen, M. (2015) 'Aristotle on knowing natural science for the sake of living well', in Henry and Nielsen, 214–31.

Levinson, R. (1953) *In Defense of Plato*. Cambridge.

Lockwood, T. (2019) 'The best way of life for a polis (*Politics* VII.1–3)', *Polis* 36: 5–22.

Lockwood, T. and Samaras, T. eds. (2015) *Aristotle's Politics: A Critical Guide*. Cambridge.

Lord, C. (1982) *Education and Culture in the Political Thought of Aristotle*. Ithaca.

Mayhew, R. (1997) 'Part and whole in Aristotle's political philosophy,' *The Journal of Ethics* 1: 325–40.

McKirahan, R. (1992) *Principles and Proofs: Aristotle's Theory of Demonstrative Science*. Princeton.

McPherran, M. ed. (2010) *Plato's Republic: A Critical Guide*. Cambridge.

Miller, F. (1995) *Nature, Justice, and Rights in Aristotle's Politics*. Oxford.

Moktefi, A. (2011) 'Geometry: The Euclid debate', in Flood, Rice, and Wilson, 320–36.

Moore, C. (2019) 'Aristotle on *Philosophia*', *Metaphilosophy* 50: 339–60.

Morrison, D. (2001) 'The happiness of the city and the happiness of the individual in Plato's *Republic*', *Ancient Philosophy* 21: 1–24.

Morrison, D. (2013) 'The common good', in Deslauriers and Destrée, 176–98.

Morrison, D. (2017) 'Aristotle on the happiness of the city', in Bermon, Laurand and Terrel, 11–24.

Nagel, T. (1980) 'Aristotle on *eudaimonia*', in Rorty, 7–14.

Neu, J. (1971) 'Plato's analogy of state and individual: The *Republic* and the organic theory of the state', *Philosophy* 46 (177): 238–54.

Newman, W. ed. (1887/1902) *The Politics of Aristotle*. 4 Vols. (I–II: 1887, III–IV: 1902). Oxford.

Nightingale, A. (2004) *Spectacles of Truth in Classical Greek Philosophy*. Cambridge.

Notomi, N. and Brisson, L. eds. (2013) *Dialogues on Plato's Politeia (Republic)*. Sankt Augustin.

Nussbaum, M. (1988) 'Nature, function, and capability: Aristotle on political distribution', *Oxford Studies in Ancient Philosophy*. Suppl. Vol. 145–84.

Ostenfeld, E. ed. (1998) *Essays on Plato's Republic*. Aarhus.

Pellegrin, P. (2015) 'Is politics a natural science?' in Lockwood and Samaras, 27–45.

Popper, K. (1966) *The Open Society and Its Enemies*, Vol. 1: *The Spell of Plato*, 5th ed. London.

Rabinoff, E. (2019) Review of Matthew Walker, *Aristotle on the Uses of Contemplation*. *Ancient Philosophy* 39: 484–89.

Reeve, C. D. C. trans. (1998) *Aristotle: Politics*. Indianapolis.

Robinson, T. (1967) 'Soul and immortality in *Republic* X', *Phronesis* 12: 147–51.

Robinson, R. ed. (1995) *Aristotle: Politics, Books V and VI*. Rev. ed. Oxford.

Roochnik, D. (2008) 'Aristotle's defense of the theoretical life: Comments on "Politics" 7', *Review of Metaphysics* 61: 711–35.

Rorty, A. ed. (1980) *Essays on Aristotle's Ethics*. Berkeley.

Rosler, A. (2013) 'Civic virtue: Citizenship, ostracism, and war', in Deslauriers and Destrée, 144–75.

Ross, W. D. ed. (1949) *Aristotle's Prior and Posterior Analytics*. Oxford.

Ross, W. D. trans. (1984) *Aristotle's Nicomachean Ethics*. Rev. Urmson, J. in Barnes, II 1729–1867.

Ross, W. D. trans. (1984a) *Aristotle's Metaphysics*, in Barnes, II 1552–1728.

Rowe, C. (1991) 'Aims and methods in Aristotle's *Politics*', in Keyt and Miller, 57–74.

Rufener, R. and Szlezák, T. eds. (2003) *Platon: Der Staat*. Düsseldorf and Zürich.

Sachs, J. trans. (2007) *Plato: Republic*. Newburyport.

Salkever, S. ed. (2009) *The Cambridge Companion to Ancient Greek Political Thought*. Cambridge.

Salkever, S. (2009a) 'Reading Aristotle's *Nicomachean Ethics* and *Politics* as a single course of lectures: Rhetoric, politics, and philosophy', in Salkever, 209–42.

Saunders, T. ed. (1995) *Aristotle Politics: Books I and II*. Oxford.

Schleiermacher, F. trans. (1828) *Platon: Der Staat*. Berlin.

Schleiermacher, F. and Chambry, É. trans. (1971) *Platon: Der Staat.* Rev. Kurz, D. Darmstadt.

Schmelzer, C. ed. (1884) *Platos ausgewählte Dialoge*, Vol. 7. *Der Staat.* Berlin.

Schofield, M. (2006) *Plato: Political Philosophy.* Oxford.

Schofield, M. (2006a) 'Aristotle's political ethics', in Kraut, 305–22.

Scott, D. (1999) 'Aristotle on well-being and intellectual contemplation', *Proceedings of the Aristotelian Society.* Suppl. Vol. 225–42.

Scott, D. (2008) 'Plato's *Republic* ', in Fine, 360–82.

Scott, D. (2015) *Levels of Argument: A Comparative Study of Plato's Republic and Aristotle's Nicomachean Ethics.* Oxford.

Scott, D. (2020) *Listening to Reason in Plato and Aristotle.* Oxford.

Scott, D. (2021) 'Natural born philosophers', in Adamson and Rapp, 35–58.

Sedley, D. (2007) 'Philosophy, the forms, and the art of ruling', in Ferrari, 256–83.

Segev, M. (2017) 'Aristotle on group agency', *History of Philosophy Quarterly* 34: 99–113.

Shorey, P. trans. (1937) *Plato: The Republic.* 2 Vols. Cambridge.

Smith, N. (2010) 'Return to the cave', in McPherran, 83–102.

Solmsen, F. (1964) 'Leisure and play in Aristotle's ideal state', *Rheinisches Museum für Philologie* 107: 193–220.

Solmsen, F. (1975) *Die Entwicklung der aristotelischen Logik und Rhetorik.* Zurich.

Spelman, E. (1983) 'Aristotle and the politicization of the soul', in Harding and Hintikka, 17–30.

Szabó, A. (1978) *The Beginnings of Greek Mathematics*, trans. Ungar, A. Dordrecht.

Szlezák, T. (1976) 'Unsterblichkeit und Trichotomie der Seele im zehnten Buch der *Politeia*', *Phronesis* 21: 31–58.

Taub, L. (2003) *Ancient Meteorology.* London.

Taylor, C. (1990) 'Aristotle's epistemology', in Everson, 116–42.

Vegetti, M. (2013) 'How and why did Plato's *Republic* become apolitical?' in Notomi and Brisson, 3–15.

Vlastos, G. (1995) 'The theory of social justice in the *polis* in Plato's *Republic*', in *Studies in Greek Philosophy*, ed. Graham, D. Vol. II (Princeton) 69–103.

Walker, M. (2018) *Aristotle on the Uses of Contemplation.* Cambridge.

Waterfield, R. trans. (1993) *Plato: Republic.* Oxford.

Wilkes, K. (1980) 'The good man and the good for man in Aristotle's ethics', in Rorty, 341–58.

Woolf, R. (2012) 'How to see an unencrusted soul', in Barney, Brennan and Brittain, 150–73.

Acknowledgements

Unless stated otherwise, translations of the *Republic* are by Shorey (1937) and translations of Aristotelian works are from Barnes (1984), both with occasional modifications. I have transliterated some Greek words but avoided transliterating phrases and whole sentences (which is disorientating for those who know Greek and pointless for those who do not).

I would like to thank Michael Sharp and the production team at CUP for their speed and efficiency. James Warren, editor of the series, has been an invaluable help, and I have benefitted greatly from all the reviewers' comments.

Parts of this Element were given as talks at conferences in St Andrews and Athens. I would like to thank the participants for their feedback. I am also grateful also to Laura Biron-Scott, Hermann Cruewell, Terry Irwin and Guy Westwood for discussion of individual points.

About the Author

Dominic Scott is a Professor of Philosophy at the University of Oxford. He was a Lecturer in Philosophy at Cambridge from 1989 to 2007 and a Professor at the University of Virginia from 2007 to 2014. He was written and edited several books, including two that focus on ethics and politics in Plato and Aristotle: *Levels of Argument: a Comparative Study of Plato's Republic and Aristotle's Nicomachean Ethics* (2015), and *Listening to Reason in Plato and Aristotle* (2020).

Cambridge Elements ≡

Ancient Philosophy

James Warren

University of Cambridge

James Warren is Professor of Ancient Philosophy at the University of Cambridge. He is the author of *Epicurus and Democritean Ethics* (Cambridge, 2002), *Facing Death: Epicurus and his Critics* (2004), *Presocratics* (2007) and *The Pleasures of Reason in Plato, Aristotle and the Hellenistic Hedonists* (Cambridge, 2014). He is also the editor of *The Cambridge Companion to Epicurus* (Cambridge, 2009), and joint editor of *Authors and Authorities in Ancient Philosophy* (Cambridge, 2018).

About the Series

The Elements in Ancient Philosophy series deals with a wide variety of topics and texts in ancient Greek and Roman philosophy, written by leading scholars in the field. Taking a theme, question, or type of argument, some Elements explore it across antiquity and beyond. Others look in detail at an ancient author, a specific work, or a part of a longer work, considering its structure, content, and significance, or explore more directly ancient perspectives on modern philosophical questions.

Cambridge Elements ⹀

Ancient Philosophy

Elements in the Series